WHAT'S YOUR PRESENTATION PERSONA?

WHAT'S YOUR

PRESENTATION

PERSONA?

DISCOVER YOUR UNIQUE COMMUNICATION STYLE AND SUCCEED IN ANY ARENA

SCOTT SCHWERTLY
and
SUNDAY MANCINI

Mc
Graw
Hill
Education

NEW YORK   CHICAGO   SAN FRANCISCO   ATHENS
LONDON   MADRID   MEXICO CITY   MILAN
NEW DELHI   SINGAPORE   SYDNEY   TORONTO

1 2 3 4 5 6 7 8 9   LCR   22 21 20 19 18 17

ISBN 978-1-259-86063-8
MHID   1-259-86063-9

e-ISBN 978-1-259-86064-5
e-MHID   1-259-86064-7

Library of Congress Cataloging-in-Publication Data

Names: Schwertly, Scott, author. | Mancini, Sunday, author.
Title: What's your presentation persona? : discover your unique communication
   style and succeed in any arena / by Scott Schwertly and Sunday Mancini.
Description: 1 Edition. | New York : McGraw-Hill Education, 2017.
Identifiers: LCCN 2016039506 (print) | LCCN 2016053038 (ebook) | ISBN
   9781259860638 (hardback) | ISBN 1259860639 (hardback) | ISBN 9781259860645
   () | ISBN 1259860647
Subjects: LCSH: Business presentations. | Business communication. | BISAC:
   BUSINESS & ECONOMICS / Business Communication / Meetings & Presentations.
Classification: LCC HF5718.22 .S357 2017 (print) | LCC HF5718.22 (ebook) |
   DDC 658.4/52--dc23
LC record available at https://lccn.loc.gov/2016039506

McGraw-Hill Education books are available at special quantity discounts to use as premiums and sales promotions or for use in corporate training programs. To contact a representative, please visit the Contact Us pages at www.mhprofessional.com.

To my son, Stone,
for being my inspiration for everything I embrace and chase.
You provide purpose and meaning to all of my life's work.
—SS

To Valerie, Lauren, and Parissa,
for your inspiration, wit, and patience. I couldn't have done it
without those long walks and all of your friendship.
—SM

CONTENTS

PART II: THE 4 QUADRANTS

ACKNOWLEDGMENTS

This beautiful project has been a significant part of both our lives for close to two years now. As Steve Jobs once put it:

> The only way to be truly satisfied is to do
> what you believe is great work. And the only way to do
> great work is to love what you do.

We couldn't agree more. This was an absolute labor of love. From idea to finished page, this project has been an amazing ride. Sure, we cried a little and bled a little along the way, but it was a wonderful journey seeing this book come to life.

We have so many people to thank for helping us get to the finish line. We wouldn't be here without you. Thanks to our fellow Ethos3 and Badge task force members Valerie Gepner, Lauren Paxton, and Cara Schwertly. Your contributions to this project have been absolutely amazing. Valerie, you did such a fantastic job with the design (a shout-out to Kyle Scudder as well). Lauren, your tireless efforts behind the scenes, testing again and again, is truly appreciated. Cara, this concept would have never had wings without your genius.

We would also like to thank Chad Lightner for taking our vision and making it a reality online. You worked diligently behind the scenes to create a beautiful assessment that really shines. Thanks to Herb Dew for sharing with us the power of assessments. We would also like to thank Casey Ebro, our editor at McGraw-Hill. Thank you for believing in us and our idea. It's been an absolute pleasure working with you on this project. A big shout-out to Linda Konner. You are an amazing agent. You believed in us from day one, and for that we are eternally grateful.

Finally, we would like to thank our friends and families. Without your support, none of this could have happened. We love you, we thank you for your patience, and we look forward finally to getting to spend time with you now.

WHAT'S YOUR PRESENTATION PERSONA?

Introduction

WHAT IS BADGE?

W e're ecstatic that you are taking this first big step to learn more about yourself and your personal presentation style. Thank you for making an investment in you. We're confident that what you will find in these pages will change the way you approach presentations for the rest of your life. We are looking forward to being part of this journey of discovery with you.

Look around you.

The world is brimming with presenters who need coaching and direction. They seem unaware, almost zombielike. They haven't tapped into their strengths. They are unaware of how to manage their weaknesses. Most important, they don't know how to create and design a presentation that fits their true style. Their presentations serve as testaments that it is a jungle out there filled with Death by PowerPoint. According to Microsoft[1] estimates, 30 million presenters take the stage every single day, bringing audiences to what feels like the Land of Nowhere. We all know what those presentations look and sound like: a bit painful on the eyes and ears.

We applaud you in your decision to be different as you seek to grow and challenge yourself to be a better public speaker and presenter. Your next talk is an opportunity to inspire, educate, or even change the world. And that is why we are so thrilled you decided to pick up a copy of *What's Your Presentation Persona?* We believe with all our hearts that you have in your hands a tool that will change forever the way you give your future presentations. You have in your possession a ticket to an entirely new world.

It will give you the gift of self-awareness.

It's the one trait that separates the successful from the unsuccessful, the paint-by-number hobbyist from the professional artist. We wish our business culture would pay more attention to this. We hold work traits such as responsibility, initiative, and drive dear, but too often we neglect this vital component.

As a business owner and manager of people and teams, this is the trait I (Scott) value most. I never expect anyone to be a master of many tasks. In fact, I would rather have a team member be a master of one task than be mediocre at many. I want the amazing salespeople with no expectation that they can manage projects. I want the highly creative designers with no expectation that they can lead a team. I want the dynamic content strategists with no expectation that they can negotiate with clients. I want people who are self-aware, who know their strengths and can manage their weaknesses so that they can work at their very best.

THE BEAUTY OF SELF-AWARENESS

Having self-awareness is like having a solid investment retirement account. It's not mandatory when you are 25, but if you have one, you are set for the rest of your life. Do you know people who can't decide what they want to order from a menu, much less what they want to do for the next few years? How about the people who know what they want and have a five-year plan? The former suffers from a deficiency of self-awareness, while the latter does not.

Being self-aware means the following:

- You know who you are at your core.

- You know what motivates you and what will put a fire in your belly.

- You know how to control your emotions and master your feelings.

- You know your own strengths and how to double down on them.

- You know your own weaknesses and how to manage them.

- You know what to say and when to say it.

- You know where you can add value.

Self-awareness is a beautiful thing.

WHERE IT ALL STARTED

At our presentation training and design firm, Ethos3, we're huge advocates of self-awareness, so we issue the Predictive Index (PI) to every prospective employee. The Predictive Index is the grandfather of the Myers-Briggs Type Indicator (MBTI) assessment, and it predicts your personality profile. It's very similar to the Dominance Influence Steadiness Conscientiousness (DiSC) assessment that measures your social tendencies (introvert versus extrovert), level of dominance (that is, type A personalities), and much more.

I (Scott) have to give credit to Sunday on this one. We were discussing personality assessments and brainstorming new initiatives in my office one afternoon.

"Why not have something like the PI for presenters?" she asked.

And so it began.

Months of trial and error. Collaboration. Research. And more research.

The result is a test drawn from over a decade of experience of building and designing presentations and training presenters all over the world: Badge.

This questionnaire was created to assess your current skills and predict your presentation style so that you can become more aware and empowered. We developed it to help presenters uncover their strengths and weaknesses so that they could prioritize which areas they need to work on.

The Badge assessment is radically honest. This information may sting, or it may empower. But in return, you will get some amazing insight and discover a completely new level of self-awareness.

An Introduction to Badge (Video):
http://ethos3.com/treats/introduction

WHAT THIS MEANS FOR YOU

Without giving away too much of our delicious secret sauce, your Badge score is calculated within the four quadrants shown in Figure I.1.

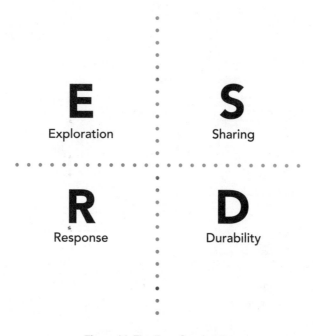

Figure I.1 The Four Quadrants

EXPLORATION

This quadrant captures everything about how you approach the task of presentation preparation. It unpacks the level of seriousness with which you plan, research, and organize your thoughts before even opening a design program such as PowerPoint.

SHARING

This quadrant measures your ability to share and deliver your message. It covers charisma, confidence, humor, authenticity, and much more. It explores just how natural or awkward you are in front of a room full of people.

RESPONSE

Do people like or dislike you once you have given a presentation? This is what the Response quadrant attempts to discover. It unpacks just how well you and your messages are received and retained by your audience.

DURABILITY

This quadrant is all about lifetime value. Does your content stand the test of time? Speeches that would score well here include Martin Luther King, Jr.'s "I Have a Dream" speech and Franklin Delano Roosevelt's Pearl Harbor address to the nation.

DON'T SETTLE WITH YOUR PRESENTATIONS

It's time to throw all of your bad habits into a large trash bag. This book is for people who don't settle, because here's the honest truth: if you aren't among the best in your organization or in your field, you are in a dangerous situation. Just getting by isn't going to cut it. A presentation is a make-or-break moment and an opportunity to stand out from everyone else who thinks clip art is acceptable and that presentation rehearsal is optional.

This book and Badge exist to achieve one goal: to make you a better presenter. They are not designed to make you a better cook, a better spouse, or even a better manager, although you may find yourself naturally improving in those areas because of your heightened self-awareness and improved presentation skills.

In these pages, you'll find our original, proprietary, one-of-a-kind presentation assessment; helpful tips and tricks; absolute clarity on the strengths and weaknesses of your public speaking style; and a better understanding of your team's speaking skills. We will help you discover your true presentation style, and we will provide ways for you to maximize your style moving forward.

If you are willing to look inward, take your profile seriously, and work hard, you just might see some fantastic results.

You'll quickly discover what strategies work best for you when preparing your message and sharing it onstage, as well as details such as which audiences are likely to adore you or be unmoved by you and how to prepare for those situations.

We have also provided you with complete access to a plethora of additional resources that you can find online at ethos3.com/treats. Feel free to visit specific links as you choose throughout your engagement with this book.

Are you ready?

Chapter 1

EXPLORING THE PROFILES

W e want to lay everything on the table right now: there is no perfect Badge profile. They all have their own strengths and weaknesses. Whether you are a C-suite executive or the office intern, there is a Badge profile for you, along with ways to improve. Your responsibility moving forward is to embrace the one you have and maximize its full potential.

You are going to discover 16 unique profiles. Each brings something different and powerful to the world of presenting. The big question is, which one best fits you? You might think of it as a row of 16 different sweaters in a variety of patterns and colors. All of these sweaters can keep you warm, but only one is in your size and fits your personal style. So which will you be?

The Activator: a dominant personality with the gift of persuasion

The Advocator: a tenacious personality with a strong purpose that drives each word

The Befriender: a charming speaker who wins over the audience time and time again

The Captivator: a charismatic presenter with a natural, unrehearsed flair

The Creator: a forward-thinking innovator energized by the next big thing

The Curator: a highly-prepped presenter who knows how to craft an enduring message

The Demonstrator: a well-rehearsed character who always takes center stage

The Director: a respected leader with an empathetic core

The Educator: an esteemed teacher who is comfortable tackling tough messages

The Liberator: an optimistic visionary who loves to inspire

The Navigator: a focused self-motivator whose goal is to get the job done right the first time

The Performer: a one-person show who can transform any dull message

The Producer: a successful speaker who believes in hard work—not luck

The Scholar: an always-curious intellectual backed by his or her own wisdom

The Scientist: an inquisitive learner who puts an emphasis on preparation and research

The Soldier: a dedicated personality driven by a single-minded, world-changing purpose

You can find all 16 in Figure 1.1—a fancy cheat sheet just for you.

Are you curious about your own profile? We are excited for you, and can't wait for you to jump in and learn more about your presentation style.

Take the Badge assessment. Here's how:

1. Go to ethos3.com/badge.

2. Complete the form.

3. Look for an e-mail from us containing your access code.

4. Click on the link provided in the e-mail to utilize your code and take the assessment.

5. Celebrate!

CHEAT ▷ SHEET

ACTIVATOR

A dominant personality with the gift of persuasion

ADVOCATOR

A tenacious personality with a strong purpose that drives each word

BEFRIENDER

A charming speaker who wins over the audience time and time again

CAPTIVATOR

A charismatic presenter with a natural, unrehearsed flair

CREATOR

A forward-thinking innovator energized by the next big thing

CURATOR

A highly-prepped presenter who knows how to craft an enduring message

DEMONSTRATOR

A well-rehearsed character who always takes center stage

DIRECTOR

A respected leader with an empathetic core

EDUCATOR

An esteemed teacher who is comfortable tackling tough messages

LIBERATOR

An optimistic visionary who loves to inspire

NAVIGATOR

A focused self-motivator whose goal is to get the job done right the first time

PERFORMER

A one-person show who can transform any dull message

PRODUCER

A successful speaker who believes in hard work— not luck

SCHOLAR

An always-curious intellectual backed by his or her own wisdom

SCIENTIST

An inquisitive learner who puts an emphasis on preparation and research

SOLDIER

A dedicated personality driven by a single-minded, world-changing purpose

Figure 1.1 The 16 Profiles

Special Note. Completing the assessment in one session is preferable. The process will take you only about 10 to 12 minutes. But if you don't finish and need to come back to the assessment, that is completely fine. Just go to http://ethos3.com/login to log back in and finish the test.

Once you complete the assessment, you'll get your Badge. You'll be on your way to discovering your exact public speaking profile, along with tips specific to you, so you can maximize every presentation opportunity. You'll also learn more about which audiences will cherish you and which will challenge you. This way, you'll be prepared for anything the moment you take center stage. After you have mastered your profile, you can learn about the others to see how they complement your individual style. This will provide perfect insight for complex tasks such as team presentations.

A FEW SUGGESTIONS FOR GETTING STARTED

Before you decide to somersault headfirst into the deep end with your newfound knowledge, we have a few suggestions for you.

1. GET DISTURBED

When you think about your list of life accomplishments, most of those accolades started with a level of disturbance. Maybe you were tired of being 25 pounds overweight so you decided to hit the treadmill and never looked back. Perhaps you decided to quit your high-paying job to start a nonprofit that helps inner city kids. At some point or another, you eventually got disturbed and told yourself, "Enough is enough" or "Life is too short." You knew something had to change, so you took a deep breath and made the leap.

Maybe you haven't made that jump just yet, and that is perfectly fine. In fact, it is completely normal. After all, we are human. We all have emotions. We all have fears. We all have insecurities. All we ask is that you acknowledge that something has to change when thinking about yourself onstage. If you need an extra level of disturbance to help push you, then follow these tips:

- **Tip 1.** Be honest. Ask yourself how you really did the last time you gave a presentation. Were you better than the other presenters? If not, what needs to change for that to happen?

- **Tip 2.** Record yourself or have someone record you. Do it. You are bound to discover some flaws and weaknesses that don't settle well with you.

- **Tip 3.** Ask for feedback. If you don't want to record yourself, then ask for an honest 360 review of your presentation skills from your peers and colleagues. Do this and you'll soon find areas where you need to improve.

- **Tip 4.** Analyze. Jump on YouTube or TED and discover speakers who are leaps and bounds ahead of your current skill set. They are normal folks just like you, so there is no reason you can't become as good as they are.

- **Tip 5.** Stop making excuses. If you are a terrible presenter, then embrace that reality right now, stop blaming others or your calendar, and focus on getting better.

If this book is in your hands, then you are already feeling disturbed. That's a good thing. Hopefully, you want to improve how you give presentations or how your team gives presentations. That's perfect because now you are ready to work on the next item. Just remember that your Badge is your Badge. It won't change you unless you are willing to do something with it.

2. GET ENTHUSIASTIC

Your Badge also has no meaning if you don't embrace the power of enthusiasm. It's every great presenter's magic weapon. Back in 2012, I (Scott) did my very first Ironman. This was a triathlon, and the day consisted of a 2.4-mile swim, followed by 112 miles on a bike and a 26.2-mile run.

I still remember the day clearly. I woke up at 4:15 a.m. to head to the Louisville Waterfront Park to await a 7 a.m. jump into the Ohio River for a long morning swim to kick off the event. That hot August day was long, brutal, and extremely mentally challenging. I counted every stroke on the swim, every pedal on the bike, and every stride on the run as my battered body worked its way to the finish line in downtown Louisville.

Thinking back to that moment at the finish line, there was one quality that helped me make it through: enthusiasm. Just a short four months earlier, I had tried my first Ironman, and I had a did not finish (DNF). I didn't even make it to the run that day, and I was forced to exit the course halfway on the bike portion because of a slow bike time. I was embarrassed. Friends and family had flown all the way to St. George, Utah, only to see me not finish. So on that sweltering day in Louisville, Kentucky, I was just happy to be there competing. Enthusiasm was bountiful that day. Cheering spectators, my friends and family, and my own enthusiasm carried me despite all the pain and discomfort.

When my spirits sagged on the bike, enthusiasm made me optimistic. When my energy levels were depleted on the run, enthusiasm helped me get a second wind. When I wanted to give up, other athletes and spectators shouted for me to "keep going." It helped me and my fellow competitors get to the finish line.

In the following weeks or months, you may find yourself having to give a presentation to a roomful of 1,000 people or maybe just 10. The demands of your day, your travel schedule, or the presentation itself may already be burdening you, but you must overcome these obstacles. Enthusiasm matters. It's a direct reflection of your heart, your passion, and your conviction. The more enthusiastic you are, the more you show that you care about the topic and your audience.

On a personal note, I (Scott) struggle with being enthusiastic every single day. It's a bit easier for Sunday. She always brightens up the office. Just ask any of our colleagues. Me, not so much. There are days when I have to present when I simply do not feel well, I'm in a different time zone and am suffering from lack of sleep, or I'm worried about my kid or some project at work. I completely understand. Life can get the better of us, but it is your responsibility as a presenter to create a great experience for your audience.

Being enthusiastic can be tough. But here's the good news: there are a few things you can do to trick your mind and body:

- **Tip 1.** You are in charge of your mindset. You can choose to be excited about sharing your message or you can choose to dread it. Enthusiasm is like the common cold. It is contagious. When your audience watches you share your story with emotion and energy, they will "catch" that same feeling.

- **Tip 2.** Breathe with intention. Be mindful of your breathing. Before your presentation, practice the 4 × 4 breathing technique,[1] in which you pause for four seconds, inhale for four seconds, pause at the top for four seconds, and then exhale for four seconds. Rinse and repeat before taking the stage to help you feel more calm and in control.

How to Do the 4x4 Breathing Technique (Video): http://ethos3.com/treats/4x4

- **Tip 3.** Use your hands.[2] Studies[3] show that those who use their hands while presenting are perceived as more competent and confident.

- **Tip 4.** Sleep. Yes, it sounds basic, but make sure you are well rested. Chronic sleep loss will deplete your energy, in turn, making you less dynamic when in front of a room. You have a busy and stressful life, so make sleep a priority.

- **Tip 5.** Blink less. The average human being blinks 15 times per minute.[4] The person who blinks more rapidly than this generally has something to hide or is engaging in a lie. If you want to look and be credible, then don't blink as much. The less you blink, the more confident you will feel.

Presenting will always be part of your professional journey. You are constantly selling, promoting, and marketing yourself, your business, or your cause. To achieve the best results, let's master this thing called "enthusiasm."

3. GET GRITTY

Disturbance? Check. Enthusiasm? Check. Now it is time to check off the most important item of all: grit. At Ethos3, we take our hiring process very seriously. Our process involves multiple interviews, assignments, and assessments. We want the best and the brightest, so we are all about hiring slow and firing fast when necessary.

On paper, it looks like we are obsessed with IQ, which we are. However, if you peel everything away, we care more about grit. It's embedded in our DNA, and here's why. It starts at the top.

My wife and I (Scott) joke all the time that she can kill me on any standardized test. It's the truth. I'm terrible at test taking, and I have never really seen myself as a smart guy. However, I work harder than most. I'm willing to wake up earlier, stay later, and simply grind it out longer than the competition. Since I am wired this way, I naturally look for this same mindset from my team. So when I ran across a recent study that discussed why some West Point recruits drop out when their peers press on, I was happy to discover that a lack of grit was the cause. It wasn't talent or IQ that got recruits to the finish line successfully. It was grit.

Psychologists Angela Duckworth and Martin Seligman discovered something very similar in New York City and Chicago public schools:

> Self-discipline predicted academic performance more robustly than did IQ. Self-discipline also predicted which students would improve their grades over the course of the school year, whereas IQ did not.

Figure 1.2 is a chart that breaks down the results of their study.[5] Simply put, the kids with grit were more likely to perform better and graduate. They were empowered by a challenge, like a spark striking the fuse of a rocket. Their grades just kept shooting up as they continued to push through prejudice and self-doubt.

If you are feeling inspired but don't know where to start, here are a few suggestions:

- **Tip 1.** Work harder. If you need to start your day earlier or stay later so you can get that presentation done, then do what you need to do to finish it and do it well.

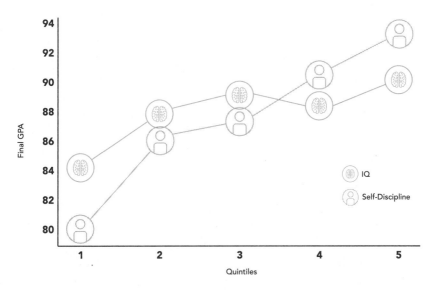

Figure 1.2 Final Grade Point Average (GPA) as a Function of
Ranked Quintiles of IQ and Self-Discipline
Source: businessinsider.com/grit-is-more-important-than-iq-2013-5.

- **Tip 2.** Work smarter. Sometimes it's not always about working harder but working smarter. Are you focusing on the right items in relation to your upcoming talk? Is your day prioritized in such a way that you are focusing on the essential rather than the nonessential?

- **Tip 3.** Don't rely on talent alone. Feel blessed that you are a natural speaker and presenter but don't rest on your laurels. Get better.

- **Tip 4.** Care more. There are too many entitled and lazy people on this earth who can't be bothered about how they look onstage. Strive for excellence.

- **Tip 5.** Be humble. Natural talent is great, but don't let it go to your head. Always remember that there is someone out there who can do your job better and faster. That person may even be a better presenter.

The lesson for all of us is this: if you think your talent or brains will always save you when you are up there onstage, think again. You need grit.

HOW TO USE THE PROFILES

 The next 16 chapters (Chapters 2 through 17) are dedicated to the profiles. If you have not taken your assessment, please do so now (http://ethos3.com/badge), and come back when you are ready to read your profile.

Then proceed to Chapter 18 through to the end of the book to learn even more about you and your presentation persona. Once you have mastered your profile, explore and experiment with the others to become a more well-rounded presenter.

You will also discover other Badge profiles that complement your style. In areas where you are weak, these natural allies are strong. The same is true for them. If you want to work on your existing weaknesses, find these corresponding personas and learn from them. They will show you what the strengths you lack look like in action, and you can do the same for them. Delivering a group presentation? Put allies on your team! Hiring someone to deliver a presentation for you? Build a team that covers all weaknesses. Your match is out there; all you have to do is say, "Hello!"

PART I

THE

16

PROFILES

———

Chapter 2

THE ACTIVATOR

MEET THE ACTIVATOR

When an Activator walks into a room, everyone knows it. That's not the opening line to a stand-up joke. It's the hard truth about one of the most exuberant and compelling personality types around. Activators get audiences energized to act on the provided call to action. Because of this raw talent, Activators make great salespeople. Smooth talking and fun to watch, that's the Activator way.

If you received the Activator as your Badge profile, you are represented by the bold falcon. This is because it's all about the hunt for you. You soar past your competition with the wind in your feathers. You're a high-energy, showy predator that dominates your natural habitat.

Your strongest natural assets are your enthusiasm for your message and your natural skill for weaving facts and stories during delivery. *Movement* is key. The driving force behind your message is to get the decision made. When a presentation ends, you also have the keen ability to socialize and make useful connections afterward.

It's not all sunshine and delicious rabbits for the falcon. You work hard at fascinating and entertaining your audience, but you also need to apply that same effort to everything else in your presentation, including rehearsal, research, and creating a message that sticks so that the audience sees you as credible. While some Activators may be practiced in adding this extra effort, others may not be so lucky.

Aside from the Performer, not many profiles have your raw talent for captivating an audience. You might not be the perfect Activator today, and maybe even the idea of getting onstage gives you an ulcer. However, the talent is there. All you need to do is work through some common failings for your type and find the right audience and platform for your message.

Let's dig a little deeper.

HOW YOU SCORED

The Activator Spotlight (Video):
http://ethos3.com/treats/activator

So how did you score the Activator? These results were calculated using our four-quadrant algorithm in which anything on the outside corner of the specific quadrant is considered high and anything near the main intersection is considered mid-low (Figure 2.1). Here is a simple rundown of your placement in each quadrant and how we arrived at your profile:

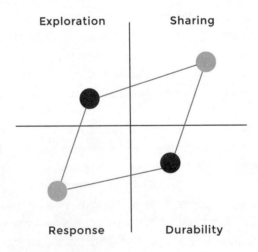

Figure 2.1 The Activator

EXPLORATION

This is the Achilles heel for Activators. They don't want to fuss with details, and they would rather wing it. You may find yourself saying, "This looks good enough," or "I don't need to practice out loud. I know how I'm going to sound." There may be some truth in this for you because your personality is strong onstage. However, don't get too comfortable. The only way your talk can achieve long-term impact is if you spend some time preparing for it.

SHARING

For every yin, there is a yang. What Activators lack in Exploration, they make up for in their onstage presence. This is the Activator's strongest category, and it is where you scored high marks to indicate your style. Most Activators are energized by their time onstage, and they come naturally equipped with a likable style that audiences enjoy. Stressful situations? No problem. Time limitations? You're not worried. A massive earthquake in the middle of your talk? You'll roll with it. Your optimism and energy make this your most powerful quadrant.

RESPONSE

Your people skills win again: this is the second-strongest scoring quadrant for Activators. You are great at networking, shaking hands, kissing babies, and answering crucial questions after your talk. Since you wield the power of a good impression, you stick in your audience's memory, at least for the short term. They might make a mental note to send you an e-mail or sign up for a newsletter after the talk. Of course, it's the Activator's duty to make sure they take this a step further, which brings us to Durability.

DURABILITY

Activators tend to score in the mid- to low range of this quadrant. But don't feel like you've received coal in your stocking; it has nothing to do with your memorable personality. This quadrant ties directly to Exploration

21

and the kinds of messages that Activators tend to choose. If they aren't planning in advance for their presentation to spread online or otherwise, then it won't have long-term weight. Activators need to think about platforms and how their message could impact an audience today and two years hence to achieve a higher Durability score. The key here is to think big and stop focusing on your artful, flashy delivery.

SPOTTING AN ACTIVATOR IN THE WILD

Let's see what an Activator looks like in action, with the tale of Martin, a man who loves nothing more than making his friends laugh and keeping spirits up at work. He is a salesman for the tech company GlowShow, which produces enormous screens for stadiums and concert venues. This means that he's on the road all the time, trying to close high-value deals with clients who may require only a one-time purchase.

Martin is a great salesperson; there's no mistaking that. He's sold a lot of expensive screens in his time at the company. But he wants to become a resource for his clients for a lifetime, selling them different tech products in the future and continuously staying top of mind. He wants to make sure his message sticks: "I am your trusted tech sales guy, forever." He wants to turn his pitch from a fling to a marriage.

The trouble with Martin is that he's not bringing the right equipment for the job. A business card gets lost, a handshake forgotten, and his single-use sales presentation is dated and focused only on one thing. So where can he start?

If the same old presentation isn't yielding different results, then Martin should have a meeting with himself in the mirror and ask, "What can I do better?" The answer is that he needs to spend time researching his competition, finding out what his audience needs, and becoming an expert in the area of sales that he wants to succeed in.

The second thing he needs to work on is his overall personal platform, which should extend far beyond a few bent business cards. With his company's approval, he could work on a landing page to show off new products, create his own blog to keep customers abreast of news, or even work on a video series to build credibility as a tech authority in the field.

Martin also needs to become a part of his clients' lives after the presentation itself, whether through an e-mail newsletter or with follow-up chats about products that he has sold. He needs to stop thinking of each short-term sale as his finish line and, instead, look toward the future in order to cultivate meaningful relationships with his clients. How can he become part of their world, not only when they need something specific from him but when they want to turn to someone for expertise? That's where persistence comes in.

Activators need to shift their lens from short distance to a much longer scope. They need to anticipate their audience's needs in the future, like viewing a battleship way out in the mist. If Martin thinks long term, his natural people skills will pair well with the Durability of his new approach. His clients will think of him in a new way, and he'll see results. Other Activator personalities can also take a lesson here, especially when it comes to developing their own platform.

With just a bit more work on the back end, Martin will sell more screens, earn more money, and make everyone happier.

YOUR NATURAL HABITAT

Activators are constantly on the go, perfectly content to hit the road, and thrilled by the idea of being center stage. You are energized by even mundane speaking events, such as giving a toast at your best friend's wedding and making an important announcement at a family gathering. Some nervous energy, sure. But this ability still offers you an upper hand against common presenter pitfalls such as stage fright and excessive self-doubt.

All you need to deliver a stunning presentation is a message to share: no expensive suit, fancy demo equipment, or magic potion required. But we recommend going a step further than this. How can you increase the size of your audience who will enjoy some of that natural energy and get even more out of your message? You can use the Internet. From podcasts to webinars to an online video series, you have everything you need to turn the entire globe into your own natural habitat.

BRAWN (STRENGTHS)

Social

Tenacious

Compelling

Most high-pressure situations and social interactions that give other presenters stress ulcers are unlikely to phase you. The thrill of the kill is what excites you. With this ability, you are a flexible and responsive speaker who can handle technological malfunctions, sleepy audiences, and more. Time constraints? No problem. Q&A sessions? You know you'll be able to answer even the toughest questions.

You're a social animal with great conversational abilities, and most people find you charming and relatable. You also understand when it's the right time to use storytelling and case studies and when it's time to switch to some facts and stats. Picking up on social cues is one of the best traits that a presenter can have, and you've got a natural radar.

TRAPS (WEAKNESSES)

Disorganized

Procrastinator

Overconfident

And now for those pesky weaknesses! Your need-for-speed attitude can sometimes lead to disorganization and an overall lack of detail. This is reflected in your score in the Exploration quadrant, where building blocks such as research, presentation design, and content all take second place to your experience onstage.

In general, Activators also tend to prefer turning the focus of a presentation on themselves rather than the core message. Confidence can be a powerful presenter's tool, but too much of it can be a turnoff for the audience. You also run the risk of sounding like a used-car salesperson if you aren't careful to back up your message with some verifiable data. But don't let that discourage you! Throw in a few facts and stats, make sure your materials look professional, and you should be able to work through any bumps.

YOUR NATURAL ALLY

Want to improve your Exploration and Durability? Connect with Scholars (Chapter 15) and take notes on how they approach each quadrant. Likewise, be sure to show them how you are a natural at Sharing and Response.

YOUR PREY

Don't let your head grow too large when we say this, but you're definitely at the top of the food chain as a presenter. Most people want to be convinced or sold, and you're the presenter for the job. Whether they are extroverts, introverts, or just a group of skeptics, your natural ability to win people over can make prey out of (mostly) anyone.

YOUR PREDATORS

Sometimes the skeptics are simply too skeptical, and your winning personality may not be enough to convince them of your message's value. Left-brain people who want to focus on a good chart rather than hear your airtight pitch will be hesitant to sign on the dotted line, for instance. Make sure you're appealing to those who may not think your jokes are funny, don't want to watch your song and dance, and probably didn't get a good night's sleep the night before. Do this by providing crucial data right away in your talk, and be careful not to exceed your time limit. Get to the point fast, and don't waste their time.

FIVE DOS AND DON'TS

DOS

1. Organize your presentation with an outline beforehand, a storyboard for your content, and at least three supporting facts or stats for each

main idea. This will help your presentation feel more credible and less "I thought of this at the last minute."

2. Avoid procrastination by using a service such as Wunderlist to create a timeline and establish due dates for your outline, initial drafts, and practice sessions. Not tough enough? Have an invested friend keep you accountable.

3. Tone down overconfident delivery by filming at least one run-through of your speech and rewatching it to make sure you come across as energetic, not aggressive.

4. Invite more people to watch your presentation: the more eyes, the better. You naturally have the energy and confidence to engage a crowd, so why hold back?

5. Since conversation and connection are your strongest assets, encourage your audience to ask questions and engage directly with you. This will enhance the overall energy of the presentation and make it much more interactive.

DON'TS

1. Don't rush your presentation because you have a lot to say and you're excited to share it. Practice with a timer beforehand and pause frequently throughout your speech.

2. You may think the design for your visuals isn't very important, but it is. Don't leave out graphics elements such as photography and typography if you are using slides. It's not always about an energetic delivery. A good design can help enforce your message.

3. Don't give all of your audiences the same presentation experience that you've delivered in the past. You may feel comfortable and confident with your current speaking style, but your audience may be looking for more. Mingle with audience members before the talk to see what they expect from you, and then travel beyond their expectations.

4. Don't veer off topic or head down too many rabbit holes during your talk. Stick to your main points and throw in a story where appropriate, but don't let your personality commandeer your presentation.

5. Don't ignore follow-up materials such as business cards and one sheets. If you want to build a lasting connection with your audience, you need to continue the conversation well past the initial delivery.

THE IDEAL ACTIVATOR

There is no such thing as a bad persona. There are only areas to improve on within your range of strengths and weaknesses. With that in mind, what do ideal Activators look like?

1. They broaden their focus from a short-term pitch to a long-term relationship with their audience.

2. They put in the extra work before their presentation even begins, realizing that a natural energy onstage and being personable just aren't enough to make a real difference.

3. They don't ever stop learning, growing, and refining their skill set.

What happens when our favorite salesperson Martin improves his natural skill set and works on each of those three core areas? The results might look a little something like this:

1. He builds meaningful relationships with his clients that create opportunities he never thought possible.

2. He works hard to create his own personal platform, which puts him far beyond the competition and his own peers.

3. He researches the current market and positions himself as an authority figure simply by becoming more knowledgeable than anyone else.

Martin is not just focused on the dollar. Instead, he is invigorated by the people-centric connections that he has cultivated. The beauty of ideal Activators is that they use their bright, lovable personalities with enough authority to make more than just a sale. The best Activators are always on target, always able to achieve what they want. Now go for it!

Chapter 3

THE ADVOCATOR

MEET THE ADVOCATOR

Advocators are on a mission to share their message, and they don't let anything stand in their way. If you received this profile, the powerful gorilla is a perfect representation of your ability to stand your ground and create experiences that last. You are often drawn to big-picture causes, and you are mighty enough to stand up to detractors and doubters. In this jungle, you're the boss.

Before they even step onstage, Advocators like you tend to choose topics that are both close to their hearts and also have long-term impact. You don't want to waste your time delivering something that has a one-time use, such as a plastic coffee pod. You want something that can become a meaningful part of your audience's life. This is why you can recognize other Advocators before you even watch their presentation: they've printed out flyers, they have a website, they run an active blog, or they have already told you all about the message in advance.

You're also much more than just a presenter with a cause. You frequently receive an energy boost from interacting with your audience on a very personal level after the talk is finished. This is because your networking and interaction skills are naturally fine-tuned to know what an audience wants to hear. If someone comes at you with a tricky question, you don't break out in a sweat. You answer eloquently and move on.

You're ready to tackle anything that happens *after* you say your final "thank you" onstage. You know how to sway people through thoughtful conversation, providing them with any next-step information to put your words to work in their lives. You would love to see your message go viral, spreading to new groups of people and taking on a life of its own. It's this beautiful, idealistic vision that endows Advocators with natural drive.

There are two troublesome issues that Advocators face. The first is the amount of work, or lack thereof, they put into preparation. Because they have so much energy for their cause, they may overlook research, rehearsal, and design in their excitement to get the message out there. Sometimes it works in their favor, and sometimes it doesn't.

The second challenge that Advocators face is their presence onstage, which can be hit-or-miss, depending on how much past experience they have. Think of it this way: you're moving through the jungle at night toward the peak of a mountain. It's a beautiful starry night, and you know that when you get to the top of this mountain, the view will be even better. Because you are focused on the mountain, looking up at the stars, and imagining how nice the view will be, . . . you keep tripping over rocks on the path. Don't let your vision and those dang stars distract you. The details matter.

Putting the extra work into your research and rehearsal will lend more credibility to your message than you realize. Either way, your audience is going to be impressed by your gorilla strength.

HOW YOU SCORED

The Advocator Spotlight (Video):
http://ethos3.com/treats/advocator

So how did you score the Advocator? These results were calculated using our four-quadrant algorithm in which anything on the outside corner of the specific quadrant is considered high and anything near the main intersection is considered mid-low (Figure 3.1). Here is a simple rundown of your placement in each quadrant and how we arrived at your profile:

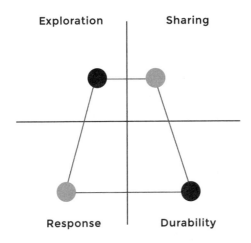

Figure 3.1 The Advocator

EXPLORATION

You scored low in this quadrant, indicative perhaps of some preexisting notions that the message is more important than the small stuff. Maybe you don't feel like slide design matters if the content is important, or perhaps you don't spend a lot of time rehearsing out loud. We pinky swear, however, that working on your level of Exploration will increase your confidence onstage and your overall impact considerably.

SHARING

Advocators score in the mid- to low range of Sharing for the same reasons that they don't spend a lot of time in Exploration. You may feel that if your message is strong enough, you won't need to fine-tune your time onstage. You also may trust in your ability to connect with others one-on-one, and you lean on this skill to help convince your audience. Either way, you aren't putting on an impressive performance. This is an area that many Advocators struggle with regularly. The key here is to focus on the details, from hand gestures to vocal tones, because all of those little nuances, when handled correctly, can add up to a much more compelling delivery.

RESPONSE

Advocators kill in this quadrant. They are careful observers of audience reaction, they invite any and all questions, and they network with gusto after the talk. They don't avoid interaction because they know they have a potent message and a passion to carry them through. Embrace this natural ability and let your group discussion overlap with the time you set aside for the talk. Tell your audience to come prepared with questions, even tough ones. You're the boss in this jungle. Don't forget it.

DURABILITY

You scored high in this quadrant, most likely because you are a big-picture person. No matter the message, you will refine it in order to last as long as possible. Like a Twinkie with no expiration date, you love listening to and delivering talks that stick around. You are also great at coming up with platforms to carry your message beyond the auditorium, using websites, blogs, or even a Twitter hashtag now and then. There's no mold on this message!

SPOTTING AN ADVOCATOR IN THE WILD

Let's see what an Advocator looks like in action, with the tale of David. David has a background in environmental policy and one huge dream: he wants to see the population of honeybees rise back to normal levels. He is working on a presentation on current local and national legislation to make people aware of the problem and to offer some practical solutions for change at the local level. He's calling it Project Save Honeybee, and he knows that it has the potential to change the world.

Here's the problem: he's so focused on the end result and the importance of this change that he doesn't realize that his delivery is awkward and his presentation looks like a 1995 PowerPoint splattered with clip art. David just assumes that people will be motivated by the global need for change, not because his deck looks pretty or he sounds slick onstage.

While the message is important, the problem is that his delivery and design seem unprofessional. Some audience members suspect that

Project Save Honeybee is a garage hobby and isn't weighty enough to throw money and time at. Even more cynical audience members suspect David himself, questioning his education and the validity of his evidence. David's project is being crushed like a bug because he has made assumptions about what the audience needs to see versus what will compel it to act.

This is a classic Advocator mistake. Everything a presenter needs for a world-changing presentation exists, but the speaker is not using all of the tools in his or her skill set to deliver it. In order to succeed, David needs to be more aware of how he comes across to his audience while he's onstage. He needs to work on his existing materials until they look professional, well researched, and attractive. And he also needs to exude confidence as he speaks, giving his audience no reason to doubt or disbelieve him.

Advocators who refocus their lens from "big picture" to "small detail" can be a powerful force for good in the world. Not only do they have the passion for a great message, they also put in all the work necessary to inspire change. With just a bit more effort, David can transform Project Save Honeybee into a presentation that his audience takes very seriously.

YOUR NATURAL HABITAT

The bigger the audience, the better. Because your messages prioritize long-term value and wide appeal, it's important that Advocators have access to a large audience. It is equally important to invite a diverse group of listeners who bring their own experiences into the room and who can help spread your message to new groups and places. Think of your message as a dandelion; you want and need for those tiny seeds to be scattered by the wind to survive.

If you can't fill a room with people or if you don't have access to a venue that will let you be heard, consider turning your presentation into a webinar or consider sharing slides and key points with others online. The Internet is one of the most powerful tools that an Advocate can use, and you are probably already using social media for promotion. Take it a step further and film your entire presentation, or create an e-mail blast with videos and a call to action. Advocators feel best when they know their message is getting out there; all they need is a little creativity and a computer.

BRAWN (STRENGTHS)

Straightforward

Persuasive

Memorable

You don't speak for anything unless you wholly believe in it, which makes you an authentic and powerful presenter. Your audience appreciates your candor and straightforward delivery style because it makes calls to action and takeaways clear and easy to digest. If they are the kind of audience that prefers a no-frills speaker, you will be incredibly persuasive.

Putting the message first does more than make you authentic. It also elevates your message as a whole. If people already know that you're selective about what you endorse, then what you say will have existing value before you even step onstage. All you need are the right words and the right materials to back your message and support the cause.

TRAPS (WEAKNESSES)

Unrehearsed

Negligent

Disconnected

The problem with prioritizing a message alone is that other aspects of a presentation fall by the wayside. It starts with a lack of preparation and research as you develop your presentation, and it may even include minimal (to no) rehearsal beforehand. Your passion may be strong, but Advocators always need to be aware that the audience might think your head is too high in the clouds to bother with the basics.

What you say may also clash with the way you are saying it. When you give a presentation, your words may say, "Take me seriously," but your body language may say, "I am not really invested in this." Yes, your message is strong, but you should still work to avoid a sloppy delivery.

YOUR NATURAL ALLY

Want to improve your Exploration and Sharing? Connect with Demonstrators (Chapter 8) and learn how they handle preparation and delivery. Likewise, be sure to share how you excel in Response and Durability.

YOUR PREY

Advocators don't have to worry about finding a special variety of prey. Anyone with spare time and a willingness to change will be interested in what you have to say, and this is especially true for audience members who don't expect to be impressed. But don't get too comfortable! Improve your odds of persuasion by adding in a dash of entertainment for performance-driven personalities and some structure for those who prefer evidence.

YOUR PREDATORS

Personalities with a short attention span, such as Performers or Captivators, will feel as if your onstage presence lacks style. You also should be wary of personalities that demand proof, such as Scientists or Liberators because most Advocators don't put enough time into research and preparation. Don't allow yourself to become the victim of doubt, like David in the example. Provide your audience with the proof and the enthusiasm it needs to believe you.

FIVE DOS AND DON'TS

DOS

1. Think like a journalist! The long-term effect of your message will be attainable only if you have the research to back up your words. Spend the bulk of your preparation time digging up trustworthy facts, stats, and other data that will give you credibility.

2. Try writing a loose script with old-fashioned pen and paper before you begin creating a full deck. We recommend picking up a Storyboard Notebook by Moleskine. This will help you slow down and focus on the correct order of the messaging, it will get you thinking about slide design, and it will put you in a mindset that makes it much easier to see the whole picture at once.

3. Words don't always speak for themselves, especially when it comes to presentations. Even though you are confident in the content of your message, always remember that delivery is just as important.

4. Spice up your delivery with relevant props, handouts, and materials that work in tandem with your message and that show your audience you put in the extra prep work for their enhanced understanding and entertainment. For instance, if you are giving a presentation about the successes and challenges of running a marathon, show your battered running shoes.

5. If storytelling scares you, you may be telling the wrong kinds of stories. Pick up a copy of Robert McKee's super helpful book *Story* for some solid examples. Get much more personal and much less confined within the subject of your presentation, and you will find that comfort follows.

DON'TS

1. Don't develop your message for a particular presentation without keeping your audience's needs in mind, especially for a specific event. Yes, your message is broadly applicable, but you should always consider options to cater specifically to their needs.

2. Don't be embarrassed to ask for design help if you need it, professionally or otherwise. There are a lot of great presentation design firms out there that can assist. Just make sure you choose one that specializes in presentation design. Many marketing and ad agencies do it, but it's not their primary service. Your message has the capability to endure, so your design should likewise be tasteful enough to outlast trends.

3. How many times do you rehearse your presentation out loud before going onstage? Don't even consider your debut until you've run through your content seven to eight times. And if it helps, rehearse so many times that you lose count.

4. Don't forget to give your audience a short-term call to action, which is something that they can accomplish shortly after the speech is finished. If everything is aimed at achieving a long-term goal, they may forget about the whole thing after a week.

5. Don't disassociate yourself from the importance of your message. If you have a viral-worthy message to share, own it. Put it on sites such as SlideShare. Become its best steward and present yourself as an authority on the subject.

THE IDEAL ADVOCATOR

There is no such thing as a bad persona. There are only areas to improve on within your range of strengths and weaknesses. With that in mind, what do ideal Advocators look like?

1. They have conducted extensive research in their topic, ensuring that they have looked at the message from all angles and can confidently offer proof points about it.

2. They know that rehearsal is a key part of their presentation's success, and they work hard to appear confident and knowledgeable while presenting onstage.

3. They work hard to become a human megaphone for their message, spreading it as far as it can go across the globe and all over the Internet.

Let's look back at David, the man who wants to save the planet one honeybee at a time. What happens when he improves? The results might look like this:

1. His materials are professionally designed and polished, with all of the information his audience needs to act on his message.

2. He makes sure that the reason his message is so important for the future is clear, using a one-two punch of storytelling and providing crucial data.

3. The audience is moved by his emotional and persuasive delivery, texting their friends about it later and trying not to let their neighbors see them tear up a little during the talk.

The result? David's incredible message goes viral online, spreading the word about Project Save Honeybee in a way that he never thought possible.

Never forget that as an Advocator, you are represented by the mighty gorilla because of your power to change the world around you for the better and to empower others with this same inner strength. Now take that message and carry it with you through the jungle and beyond. Antarctica, anyone?

Chapter 4

THE BEFRIENDER

MEET THE BEFRIENDER

E veryone loves adorable, fluffy pandas. While we're not suggesting that they are covered in fur and they eat bamboo, we *are* saying that Befrienders have strong interpersonal skills and are very well loved by their audience. This is especially true when you interact with your audience through Q&A sessions or group activities. This is because you prefer sharing the spotlight rather than keeping all of that bamboo to yourself, which is another winning characteristic of your personality.

Befrienders succeed in any area of presenting that requires a one-on-one connection. People love to voice their concerns and to feel like they're a part of the discussion. You come naturally equipped with great listening skills, and you fall perfectly into the role of a moderator or facilitator. When your audience leaves the room, they walk away with a sense of confidence about you as a person. They might not remember your key takeaways, but they will be charmed by you.

Being adorable is not enough for Befrienders to deliver a memorable, convincing presentation. They tend to struggle onstage, because of a lack of experience or a casual attitude about preparation. If pressed, most would rather schedule a long meeting or a round table discussion than spend time creating a beautiful presentation and delivering it. You can recognize this characteristic in speakers who love asking, "Does anyone have any questions so far?" after every slide that they deliver.

Another key struggle for Befrienders is achieving long-term memorability of their message. It may not even be because of the content of their talk but, rather, because they lack the confidence to be its best representative. You might not think of yourself as a great "megaphone," and perhaps you were given the task because it was necessary, not because you wanted to partake in that activity. Let us assure you: you *can* become an awesome speaker. In fact, you can become the kind of speaker whom people pay hundreds, even thousands, of dollars to watch. It just takes a little work.

To become the best Befriender you can be, the fluffy panda must move beyond likability and work toward becoming a little more intimidating. This can be accomplished with a well-researched message paired with a presentation that has been rehearsed to perfection. In short, you need to sharpen your claws.

The good news is that many presenters struggle to achieve the audience connection that comes naturally to a Befriender. Most speakers hear crickets when they try to host a Q&A, while you are always able to encourage participation and shake up the crowd. You have just enough of that special something to make each person feel that his or her opinion is valued and that he or she is truly part of the conversation. Lovable, conversational, but still needs a little work: that's the Befriender style.

HOW YOU SCORED

The Befriender Spotlight (Video):
http://ethos3.com/treats/befriender

So how did you score the Befriender? These results were calculated using our four-quadrant algorithm in which anything on the outside corner of the specific quadrant is considered high and anything near the main intersection is considered mid-low (Figure 4.1). Here is a simple rundown of your placement in each quadrant and how we arrived at your profile:

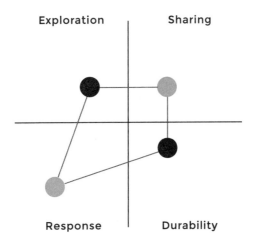

Figure 4.1 The Befriender

EXPLORATION

You scored in the mid- to low range of this quadrant, which isn't something to pop champagne about right at this moment. It doesn't mean that you don't try or you're not invested in your topic, however. Maybe you're just not sure where to start and your indecisiveness is getting you nowhere. Maybe you have a bit of self-doubt, and you just assume you'll make up for a lack of preparation during the discussion. Whatever the reason, this is one of the Befriender's weakest quadrants.

SHARING

Sharing marries perfectly with Exploration because it's a cause-and-effect relationship. Unfortunately, you scored in the mid- to low range in this quadrant as well. But don't throw this book across the room quite yet! Since you represent one of the most likable speaking personalities, developing a stronger onstage presence is a natural next step. All you need to do to improve your Sharing ability is rehearse more often, out loud, and with purpose. That's it.

RESPONSE

Now you can pop that champagne. You absolutely kill this quadrant, from mingling with your audience to making sure, at least for the short term, that they are motivated to act. You encourage discussion, assign them a task, and schedule time for some quality chitchat by the end of the session. After interacting with you, most of your audience will be sold on your message. This is due to a beautiful combination of likability and empathy on your part.

DURABILITY

Befrienders score low in Durability. Again, this is where your work in Exploration has such a huge impact. Think of your message like a seed for a perennial flower. If you plant it in the spring, you'll enjoy its beauty all summer when it blooms, but you know that it will die back in the winter frost. That's a short-term message. However, if you have built a greenhouse for the flower bed and you are fully prepared for the winter ahead, you'll enjoy the blossoms even in winter. If Befrienders put in the right prep work beforehand, their message will last longer, and their score in Durability will reflect this.

SPOTTING A BEFRIENDER IN THE WILD

What does a Befriender look like in action? Let's pick apart the story of Anne, a friendly and outgoing employee of Fine Roast, a company that roasts organic coffee beans and sells them at chains around the world. No one knows the product better than she does. She lives, breathes, and of course drinks coffee, and she knows the origin stories about the beans. The company is small, so when its main salesperson comes down with the flu, Anne is called upon to replace her and demo its latest roast flavors to one of its most important clients.

Anne's bosses have chosen her to take on this task because, frankly, they love her. She has a great sense of humor and a passion for her product. She's also worked long enough at the company to feel comfortable discussing any aspect of the Fine Roast process. When they send her to the airport with a case of new product, no one at the company is worried.

But Anne is freaking out.

Presentations are one aspect of the job that she has tried to escape at Fine Roast, which is normally a relaxed and fun place to work. She knows that she would be comfortable sitting down with the clients and sharing the new coffee, but she would not be comfortable designing a presentation and showing off some of the company's promising stats about the brand.

Because of her frustration and fear, Anne hasn't prepared anything for the meeting. Like most Befrienders, she knows she has the friendly people skills to make sure the meeting runs smoothly. But her presentation is a mess, she hasn't reviewed the info her boss told her to put in the deck, and she hasn't rehearsed at all. She assumes everything will be fine if she can just *talk* with the clients and get past all of the unnecessary corporate stuff.

It's like seeing two trains barreling toward each other, about to collide. One train is called "underpreparation," and the other is called "frustration." Anne needs to accept that presentations are a natural part of the sales process, and she also needs to have a little more faith in herself to overcome her frustration. Then she needs to practice some preparation basics, such as ensuring that her design looks sharp and professional and rehearsing her presentation out loud beforehand.

With just a little more effort and a little less fear, Anne will appear professional, prepared, and charming—and all at the same time. She doesn't have to be the bumbling yet lovable representative of her favorite brand.

Befrienders struggle when they are pushed outside of their presentation comfort zone, but it doesn't mean they need to keep struggling. They have the right personality to make a good impression. They just need to work on showcasing their best onstage, before the discussion even begins. After that, they can spend as much time as they want in the discussion phase. Anne can use that time to share coffee and ensure that the client continues a happy, long-term relationship with Fine Roast.

YOUR NATURAL HABITAT

The more intimate the group setting, the better. Befrienders like to be able to see everyone's face, measure people's reactions, and address each person specifically. They are at their best when they are the facilitators of small- to medium-size groups. They love to hear everyone's opinion and take it into serious consideration.

If possible, consider setting up the room so that you're presenting in a big circle. You can sit among your audience this way and shift the focus to the entire room rather than spotlighting yourself on a podium. This may ease a little tension and allow your best traits to shine through.

BRAWN (STRENGTHS)

Communicative

Tuned in

Altruistic

You always know what your audience wants, needs, and dreams thanks to a keen ear and great observational skills. This is paired with a genuine feeling of empathy, which is tangible when you address them. Your goal is for the audience to leave the room smiling, motivated and encouraged by the message you shared.

Even though you are a spoonful of sugar, you still know how to hold your own in conversation, whether it's a friendly debate or a question about the presentation itself. You have a broad knowledge of what you're talking about, which helps you come across as an authority during this window of time after a talk.

TRAPS (WEAKNESSES)

Underprepared

Frazzled

Short term

Befrienders tend to approach presentations with a "fly by the seat of your pants" attitude about preparation that is compounded by a dash of nervousness. This can sometimes lead to an uninspiring onstage presence that doesn't yield long-term results.

Like Anne in the example, you may feel obligated to deliver a speech or presentation that's outdated or outside your interest. However, it doesn't mean that you don't have the ability to deliver a message that's memorable or even TED worthy. The best way a Befriender can tackle these weak spots is to prepare, prepare, and then prepare some more.

YOUR NATURAL ALLY

Want to learn how to address your weaknesses? Take lessons from Producers (Chapter 14) and explore that persona to see how you can strengthen your overall strategy. While you're at it, give them a lesson in Response!

YOUR PREY

Luckily for Befrienders, your prey is pretty much everyone. You appeal to a wide range of ages, tastes, and belief systems because of your natural ability to please and your empathetic streak. However, even though your net covers wide ground, it still won't be effective if your message is shallow and forgettable. Use your charm to your advantage.

YOUR PREDATORS

Anyone in the audience who needs to be persuaded with facts and stats, such as the Scientist persona, will require you to put in extra work to be convincing. Befrienders need to make a conscious effort to build a strong call to action supported by verifiable data that causes their wise audience to *ooh* and *aah*. You should also become more mindful of your onstage presence because not all venues are ideally sized for close conversation.

FIVE DOS AND DON'TS

DOS

1. Your confidence in knowing that your audience will probably like you can lead you to scrimp on prep work. Be sure that you put in the time to research your message, design your presentation, and rehearse out loud seven to eight times.

2. Do you ever find yourself losing your main points or launching into tangents during your talk? Using a content storyboard before designing your slides can help familiarize you with the message, as well as keep you focused on your main points.

3. Since you are comfortable being the center of a conversation, work to your strengths by practicing visualization beforehand. Imagine that the audience is a group of close friends and that they are already predisposed to appreciate and enjoy what you have to say.

4. Move around onstage to give your delivery a more natural, authentic feeling. Cross from one end of the stage to the other as you make a key point, all the while maintaining eye contact with audience members.

5. Think long term! Try to connect each message you deliver to a change in your audience's life that can benefit them in the long run. It could be something small, such as reading a great book, or something much larger, such as adopting a successful habit.

DON'TS

1. Don't underestimate the necessity of supporting your main points with data that has been well researched and fact-checked. Give your message a little more meat!

2. Don't settle for a corporate or conservative design as you bring your content to life. You have the kind of presenting personality that will be best served by a fun, contemporary design that pops.

3. Don't shy away from providing your audience with handouts or other supplementary materials, especially if you tend to rush through or forget main points.

4. Don't cut back on the length of time you usually spend in discussion, group activities, or networking. That's when you shine. Use it to enrich your audience's overall experience.

5. Don't forget that social media can be a presenter's best friend. Measure the response on a presentation follow-up post and learn how to refine your message accordingly. What did your friends and fans like the most? Use that information to craft your platform.

THE IDEAL BEFRIENDER

There is no such thing as a bad persona. There are only areas to improve on within your range of strengths and weaknesses. With that in mind, what do ideal Befrienders look like?

1. They move beyond the idea that their preparation work is "good enough," and they spend time designing the deck and crafting the message.

2. They rehearse their delivery out loud, replicating the conditions of the talk as best they can to prevent presentation jitters onstage.

3. They work on making their message stick, giving their audience a reason (and proof) to heed the call to action.

What if Anna, our coffee-loving Befriender, improves her skills in each of these areas before she goes to demo the new beans? The results might look a little something like this:

1. She's less anxious presenting in front of the clients because she has run through her deck multiple times before the meeting.

2. She doesn't just appear passionate about the product. She also looks professional and ready to make the sale with the right materials to back her up.

3. She cultivates a personal relationship with the clients as a result of a great demo, and she stops fearing corporate presentations moving forward.

Great Befrienders already know they are equipped with strong people skills. You might already identify with the panda, the Badge animal that everyone wants to get close to. However, the best Befrienders know that they need to be a panda in a dress suit sometimes in order to be professional and convincing. Like Anna, they probably also need to move past misconceptions about what a presentation is capable of achieving and what their own abilities are. Sharpen those claws! Become the intimidating panda, not the one that tumbles down a slide at the zoo.

Chapter 5

THE CAPTIVATOR

MEET THE CAPTIVATOR

I n the animal kingdom, it seems like flamingos have it all. They're naturally entertaining, memorable, the bright inspiration behind lawn decor, and so much more. All they need to do is stand around sporting those hot pink feathers in order to be appreciated and loved. Captivators have a lot in common with this striking bird, as they are born with an innate sense of performance. They know how to put on a good show on and off the stage, which makes for a strong presenting style.

If you scored this personality, you can be sure that audiences already enjoy your onstage presence and remember the main points of your talk long after you step offstage. You also do a great job of facilitating discussion when necessary, carefully listening to your audience's questions and guiding them as needed. Tough questions? Rude audience members? Technical difficulties? You stand tall, and you don't let problems ruffle your feathers.

But it's not all shrimp and sunbathing for Captivators. Many rely too heavily on their natural abilities, and they avoid putting in the hard work of preparation. This can lead to a "fluffy" message that looks great and sounds great but lacks real substance. Think of an action movie with fantastic effects, hunky actors, and lots of gunpowder ... but no real plot.

Let's say you're about to deliver a big presentation about a subject you are very familiar with, given your present role. If you're already saying to yourself, "I've got this," then you may want to take a closer look at your process. Even the best can become better, and you don't want to risk coming across as cocky or as someone who is just winging the message. Are you presenting beautifully designed slides? Are you putting in the research to become an expert on your topic? Are you using tactics such as storyboarding to hone and perfect your message?

We have a hunch that you've changed your answer from "I've got this" to "hmm."

The good news is that Captivators are equipped with all the tools they need to improve their preparation and thus improve their own skills. While other presenting personalities are stressed about time onstage and flustered by Q&As, you probably won't have to face that kind of anxiety. This may be due to your existing experience, your bold personality, or your natural comfort speaking in front of others. That's why Captivators make great TED speakers, salespeople, and politicians.

Captivators dazzle the crowd with fluffy, brightly hued messages. However, you may suspect that your message doesn't have the lasting impact or persuasion power you desire. Yes, embrace your bright flamingo appeal. But make sure to do some extra prep work to catch more tasty crustaceans.

HOW YOU SCORED

The Captivator Spotlight (Video):
http://ethos3.com/treats/captivator

So how did you score the Captivator? These results were calculated using our four-quadrant algorithm in which anything on the outside corner of the specific quadrant is considered high and anything near the main intersection is considered mid-low (Figure 5.1). Here is a simple rundown of your placement in each quadrant and how we arrived at your profile:

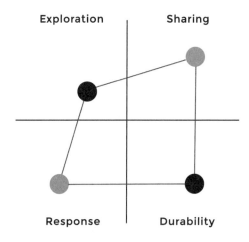

Figure 5.1 The Captivator

EXPLORATION

We'll try to let you down easy on this one: exploration isn't your strongest quadrant. In fact, it's the only quadrant where you scored in the mid- to low range. Is it a result of excessive confidence? A lack of training? Are you not sure where to begin when it comes to preparation? Whether it's one of these reasons or a souplike mixture of all three, most Captivators need to revise their Exploration approach. A convincing argument is built from the ground up, not with fancy footwork onstage. Spend more time with your message, rehearse even when you don't feel like you need to, and work on researching competitors in your field. The more you explore, the more your audience will want to explore your message as well.

SHARING

As implied by the name, Captivators shine in sharing. You scored in the high range of this quadrant, indicating a natural comfort onstage that makes most other personalities green with envy. But as with life itself, even the best could become better. Have you ever considered hosting a constructive feedback session with your team members, internally? You might be surprised to learn what areas of your delivery need improvement.

RESPONSE

Response ties heavily into the Sharing quadrant because they both require the right people skills and positive energy to excel. Once again, you scored in the mid- to high range of this quadrant because of your natural ability to please a crowd. You are the kind of baby-kissing politician whom people love to talk to after a speech, and you don't mind putting in the work to network and maintain relationships made during and after your message. However, let us be the voice that whispers in your ear, "The best can become better!"

DURABILITY

Lucky, lucky! Captivators also score in the mid- to high range of this quadrant, ensuring that their message lives on by featuring a larger platform or a call to action that really sticks. However, you can always go bigger and find more creative ways to share your message as technology changes. Take your captivating charm to the Internet and beyond, no matter what the latest social media fad may be right now.

SPOTTING A CAPTIVATOR IN THE WILD

Now that you know how you scored, it might be helpful to put everything together and see what we're talking about in a real-life scenario. Let's examine the tale of Nina, a sales executive at a company that she cofounded called Jupe Verte. This French-inspired lifestyle boutique sells home goods at its main location in San Diego and smaller locations around the country. Nina is passionate about the beautiful objects she sells and the country that inspired it, which has made her an incredible sales executive as the company has expanded over the years.

When Nina makes a sales pitch, she brings a whole treasure chest of sample products and French treats for the potential client to enjoy. Her excitement for her work is infectious, and she also does an excellent job of cultivating long-term relationships with buyers. It is her dream to see Jupe Verte boutiques across the entire country, bringing a bit of French charm to American homes.

It's hard not to love Nina. She likes to toss around French expressions, and she wears an all-white linen suit as if she's about to hop on a private jet to the countryside right after each meeting. She's the perfect example of Captivators who have worked on their personal brand and feel incredibly comfortable doing what they do best.

In spite of all these wonderful characteristics working for Nina, she could still do much better. She's so focused on French trends and what's working in the European market that she waves off the idea of doing a deep study of what Americans need. Because of this, buyers feel that Jupe Verte is too niche to expand in a much bigger way in the United States.

Nina needs to put her passion aside for a moment and use research to face truths she might not want to explore. It's like she is wearing blinders. On the left side, her vision is blocked by her past experience that keeps her motivated to stay on track. On the right side, her own passion prevents her from examining what other buyers might be looking for or what needs might not be being met in the current market.

In short, she needs to do her homework. Nina may be missing sales opportunities. She needs to spend time questioning her own tried-and-true process to see if there are changes she could make to grow the brand she loves even further.

Many Captivators are like Nina: either they feel like they have it all or they feel like they are well on their way to becoming a success by relying on natural talent. Let this assessment be the foghorn that tells you there are still ways to improve, particularly in the area of Exploration. If Nina takes the time to revise her sales strategy before she even steps into a room, Jupe Verte has a chance to dominate the market and expand.

YOUR NATURAL HABITAT

Captivators are fearless in the face of audiences large and small, so you don't have to worry about choosing a venue size to match your style. Any room will do! However, we recommend that you do not limit yourself to a conference room with five chairs. A long-term message calls for a larger audience, so try to find ways to grow your audience, whether by incorporating a live webinar or by offering an encore presentation to different groups after the initial one.

In general, Captivators also perform best when they limit their speaking time. If they find that most of their messages succeed without much prep work, then the quicker and more concise their message, the better. Any longer and the audience will start to wonder about the proof behind the beautiful display.

BRAWN (STRENGTHS)

Flashy

Memorable

Fearless

Being strong at delivery doesn't just mean you do a great job onstage. It also refers to all the networking and time spent catering personally to audience needs after the talk. Captivators are great at all of it, and they make a fantastic impression wherever they go. Their messages are also highly customized to audience needs, which means they are appreciated long after the talk itself.

Personal branding and style are also a huge part of being a Captivator. Like Nina in our example, you have spent a long time crafting your persona. It's a role that you are comfortable adopting onstage, and it makes you memorable. You aim to please, and you do it well.

TRAPS (WEAKNESSES)

Flimsy

Unprepared

Sedentary

As you can deduce from the overview, Captivators struggle with preparation. They often find themselves thinking, "If it ain't broke, why fix it?" This can sometimes put them in a tight spot when a hard-hitting question is asked or something unexpected occurs. Even worse, audience members may question your credibility if they don't feel that you've put in enough research to present yourself as an authority.

It's also easy for Captivators to let slide certain aspects of their presentations, mostly due to their own confidence. If you're not open to changing your practice routine (or lack thereof), you might be stuck with the same display of skills over and over again ad infinitum.

YOUR NATURAL ALLY

Want to improve Exploration? Connect with Scientists (Chapter 16) to learn how they prepare for a presentation, and take some serious notes!

YOUR PREY

People like to leave the room with a nugget of wisdom that makes them feel informed and good about the world. This could be something to act on in the short term, such as downloading an app, or in the long term, such as adopting a healthy new habit. The good news for Captivators is that they appeal to both personalities, and they just need to put in a little research to discover what that specific audience may be looking for before the talk.

YOUR PREDATORS

Your predators are those who don't just want to see the answer to the math problem. They want to be shown your entire process. They are personalities who question everything, not just your message, such as Scientists and Curators. You'll recognize these types by their quizzical expressions as they listen to your talk, followed by a swiftly raised hand during the Q&A. Make sure you've done your homework and you'll be able to satisfy them.

FIVE DOS AND DON'TS

DOS

1. Steer clear of the feeling that your natural skills are all you need to deliver a presentation. Even natural communicators can get better.

2. Take inspiration from other speakers you love, whether corporate or on the TED stage, and do some research to learn their preparation routines. What can you copy? How can you incorporate their routines into your own prep work?

3. Schedule more time to work on the storyboard of your presentation before an event. This includes time spent researching your topic, looking through relevant quotes and materials, and editing your on-slide copy so it comes across as clean and professional.

4. Use slides to emphasize your most important points. Put one high-level concept from your talk on each slide and then practice delivering the presentation alongside these clear points. This will help keep you on track during your talk and prevent you from going off on tangents.

5. Give yourself plenty of time after a presentation to mingle, ask your audience questions, and engage in other one-on-one activities to make them feel valued and drive home your message even more.

DON'TS

1. Don't be afraid to let your personality shine through. No matter how corporate or professional your audience may be, they will love to be entertained by you.

2. Don't forget to customize your message to the specific audience you are speaking to, which you can accomplish with a little bit of good old-fashioned research.

3. Don't underestimate your audience's ability to detect when you haven't put in the work. Show your sources, including those for your quotes, and make sure that your data is supportive of your message.

4. Don't stay stagnant! No matter what your level of experience delivering presentations is, change your usual rehearsal process by asking a friend for feedback, practicing out loud, and rehearsing in the venue itself before the event.

5. Don't forget to give your audience a clear call to action at the end of your presentation that tells them exactly what to do when you're done. Your audience will need a course of action at the end of the talk no matter how fun your delivery was.

THE IDEAL CAPTIVATOR

There is no such thing as a bad persona. There are only areas to improve on within your range of strengths and weaknesses. With that in mind, what do ideal Captivators look like?

1. They look past their own experience and confidence to address underlying habits that may hold them back.

2. They constantly look for ways to improve the little things about their presentation, from better design to deeper content.

3. They kick their ego in the knees and look at each speaking opportunity as a brand-new challenge to their existing skills and ability.

What happens when Nina, our favorite Francophile, applies some of these lessons to become an ideal Captivator?

1. She revisits her long-term strategy for Jupe Verte by devoting time to market research, ensuring that she knows the needs of U.S. consumers.

2. She is able to use her revised strategy to grow Jupe Verte in ways she didn't expect, all because of her fresh approach.

3. She comes across as more than just an energetic, memorable presenter: she becomes more credible to her potential clients.

Captivators already know that they are going to do a fantastic job at entertaining their audience. But ideal Captivators are able to dig deeper within themselves, far beyond the flashy pink flamingo feathers. They realize that Exploration (preparation) before delivery can make the difference between a message that is fun for an audience and one that has a long-lasting, meaningful impact. If you are feeling a tiny pinch of guilt in your stomach as you review the Exploration questions and recommendations, give that guilt a hug and say to yourself, "We've got a little more work to do."

Chapter 6

THE CREATOR

MEET THE CREATOR

Like the resourceful beaver, Creators can transform a few twigs and leaves into something incredible. Even better, they don't need a blueprint to do it; they exhibit a natural know-how. Most Creators are inventors, entrepreneurs, or "new-toy" kind of thinkers. They are able to take inspiration from the most unlikely places, and they feel a natural energy to start and then build a long-lasting dam that the entire forest can appreciate.

If you received this profile, you are probably fueled by new ideas with an excitement that can be seen from the moon. This joy influences the way you consume and share information, especially onstage. You can easily recognize Creators by their natural speaking energy, not because they love presenting but because they love talking about innovative ideas. In all aspects of their lives, they frequently share world-changing, groundbreaking, interesting information with those around them.

Creators aren't limited to a perpetual internal stream of "shiny new objects!" They also have a strong amount of empathy for their audience, and they love to see positive change in those around them. This is why they strive to choose messages that have long-lasting impact. They want to see positive change happen in the world. This perspective gives Creators a terrific onstage presence with enduring appeal.

However, the course of a river doesn't always run smoothly for Creators. This persona tends to struggle with details, lacking the energy or desire to spend time in the research phase once they've started building on a great idea. They also tend to avoid connecting with their audience offstage, shying away from discussion sessions that might dampen their adventurous spirit. Creators don't like people who wear frowns and ask a lot of questions.

Think about the last time you had dinner with friends, and all of you talked about what you were working on or were interested in. The conversation was lively; your friends probably enjoyed seeing that sparkle in your eyes, and you felt great sharing something new. Creators' presentations are a lot like that: casual and fun. The core problem occurs when your friends become audience members, and those audience members are looking for proof points in order to believe you're a credible presenter.

Ideal Creators don't just follow their internal blueprint. They are sophisticated enough to know that other preparatory work needs to be done in order to build the right foundation. Let's take a more in-depth look at exactly what we mean.

HOW YOU SCORED

The Creator Spotlight (Video):
http://ethos3.com/treats/creator

So how did you score the Creator? These results were calculated using our four-quadrant algorithm in which anything on the outside corner of the specific quadrant is considered high and anything near the main intersection is considered mid-low (Figure 6.1). Here is a simple rundown of your placement in each quadrant and how we arrived at your profile:

EXPLORATION

Creators like you score in the mid- to low range of this quadrant. It's not because you're lazy or don't care about prep work. Sometimes excitement takes over, and you don't want to risk overthinking your message

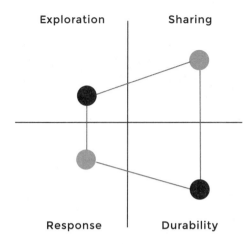

Figure 6.1 The Creator

or spending too much time fussing with the details when you know that as a whole, your presentation is going to rock. Creators often don't use a magnifying glass to review the content and design of their deck, and they don't enjoy or practice out-loud rehearsals if they can help it. We don't want to shake our fingers at you, but really, this quadrant could use some work.

SHARING

Now here is a quadrant where Creators sparkle. Your time onstage is enhanced by your own natural energy. As if you were a flower opening up to a bright day, an audience brings out your best qualities. Unlike many different presenter personalities, you can transform your nervousness into energy and inspire your audience. From moving around the stage and using well-timed gestures to incorporating storytelling effortlessly to enhance your message, you own this quadrant.

RESPONSE

This is another area of weakness for Creators, who score in the mid- to low range. A lot of this comes down to post-delivery discussion, where you may feel uncomfortable with group input, question-and-answer sessions, or other interactive activities. You scored in the low range also because you aren't entirely sure how well your message was received, even after a vibrant delivery. Our best advice is to know your audience's needs and concerns before you walk into the room, which is accomplished in the research phase of Exploration. This way, you'll be more prepared to accommodate their preferences, and you will be able to deliver a talk that makes them stand up and slow clap.

DURABILITY

Durability is no concern for a Creator; your messages are built to last, and you usually share these messages through a platform (such as a newsletter, website, or podcast) that you have created or plan to create. You prefer long-term messages that equate to long-term change. Even if you're not the one delivering the talk, you hope that your message will spread beyond your soapbox. This is reflected in your score, which is in the highest range of this quadrant.

SPOTTING A CREATOR IN THE WILD

Now that you know a little bit more about the Creator, let's dive into an example so you can get an idea of your own style in action. Meet Jeff, the head of marketing at a design firm called Upsilon that creates web advertisements. He is a beloved leader, with an office filled with toys and a weekly newsletter loaded with puns and gifs that he sends to the entire office.

Jeff has recently discovered brand-new software that would make creating banner ads faster and more efficient for the design team. Even though he deals with marketing for the company, he is hugely invested in the company's productivity and happiness. This new software has set off a lightbulb in his head that blinks: "Eureka!"

The problem is that his entire firm would need to be trained in how to use this new software, which would take time away from the designers' busy schedules, which will make it much harder for Jeff to persuade the management team that the training is a good idea.

Because he is a Creator, he knows this software is a fantastic idea. He knows wholeheartedly that the entire company will save time in the long run, and he wants to do everything in his power to make this great thing happen. Jeff calls a meeting with the CEO, the entire management team, and anyone else who will listen. He's prepared a short presentation, and he is ready to pitch the design software in a brief 15-minute speech.

Jeff delivers a high-energy, convincing pitch. He waves his arms around and points at a clock to indicate how much time they are wasting with the old software versus the amount of time needed for training. His team members enjoy the pitch and personally commit to searching for more information after the talk to verify some of his key points.

But Jeff could have done better. He has a hard time answering direct questions after his talk, mostly because he didn't spend enough time researching the technical aspects of the software. His slides were thrown together an hour before the meeting, and they didn't include the kind of data that would convince someone like the CFO. And finally, many of his coworkers are doubting his credibility in design because his skills are rooted in marketing. It is clearly evident that he didn't put in the research to appeal to an audience that is primarily design driven.

Creators like Jeff deliver presentations every day that are fun to watch and are fueled by strong passion but don't achieve their ideal goals. With just a little more work, Jeff could have surprised his teammates with thoughtful research and the right amount of data as a form of proof. He could have prepared properly for questions and ensured that he appeared credible in front of his audience. Creators have the drive; they just need to lock down those pesky details.

YOUR NATURAL HABITAT

The audience size and venue take a backseat to the excitement you have for your message: you're comfortable in front of anyone who is willing to listen. This offers you a large advantage when it comes to presenting because you are driven by your message rather than your ego alone, and you are not afraid of talking about something you believe in passionately.

Fearless personalities driven by purpose can move mountains, especially when there is a big crowd giving them natural energy or a rush.

And since you often neglect to include Q&A sessions and activities during your talk, speaking in front of a large crowd may prevent the possibility of a discussion. You feel best when you can deliver a message, make a good impression, and mic drop before walking off the stage.

BRAWN (STRENGTHS)

Entrepreneurial

Creative

Futuristic

Creativity is a keen strength to have in the business world, and you have it in spades. Your ability to generate new ideas and focus on a long-term vision makes you an entrepreneurial figure, with the passion and persistence to back it up. Learning how to sell these golden nugget ideas is crucial: don't let all of that inventiveness go to waste!

Most audiences love to hear statements that reinforce their own beliefs or encourage them to think that they are on the right path. Making your audience experience that special warm-inside feeling is a specialty of yours. Creators easily convey that they have their audience's best interests at heart, whether now or in the future. It's a big reason you scored so highly in the Sharing quadrant.

TRAPS (WEAKNESSES)

Brazen

Reckless

Chaotic

Sometimes being focused on the big picture can cause you to lose sight of important details. This lack of specificity can be evident in your speech and in the core plan of your presented idea, which may make it appear haphazard. Because creative lightning tends to strike often and at random, you may also fall victim to choosing the wrong audience or to presenting your information at the wrong time.

As in the tale of Jeff, a lack of preparation can also diminish your credibility. Sometimes people want to see more facts than flash, and your style tends to lean toward the flashy. The best option would be to sprinkle in a little something for everyone in your audience, venturing outside of your comfort zone by adding an extra hour or two of research time in Exploration.

YOUR NATURAL ALLY

Want to learn how to strengthen your Response and Exploration? Connect with Navigators (Chapter 12)! You provide a balance to their weaknesses, and vice versa.

YOUR PREY

Other Creator types will eat your ideas up; they too love to see innovative concepts presented by an inspired and inspiring inventor. As a bonus, these audience members will tend to ask fewer questions, will require less evidence, and probably won't need to see a detailed road map.

YOUR PREDATORS

Audience members who want to see the blueprints behind your creative ideas will tend to be your biggest challenge. Experienced investors and venture capitalists (VCs), as well as detailed-oriented left-brain people, will not be impressed by energy alone. It's important that you cater your message to your predators by including tangible information: market size, timelines, strategies, and proven statistics are all great ways to enhance your message.

FIVE DOS AND DON'TS

DOS

1. Write down the big-picture idea behind your presentation and then support this premise with two to five facts. Edit these facts down to the most essential, trustworthy pieces of information and include them in your outline.

2. Make sure your big idea is grounded in something the audience can relate to in the moment. Enable them to connect your creation with what they encounter day to day.

3. Organize your speech as follows: write down all the main points you want to share on sticky notes and then use a flat surface to develop the flow from start to finish. This easy way to create a storyboard should help your speech make logical sense.

4. Be sure your presentation has a call to action that your audience can accomplish in the future or near future. Otherwise, your audience will have heard an interesting idea that they will have forgotten about a week later.

5. Allow for a Q&A session after your talk to alleviate any disbelief the audience may have. A successful Q&A will boost your authority in your field.

DON'TS

1. Don't ditch crucial fact-checking preparation time before your speech. Your idea may be strong, but your research needs to be stronger.

2. Use your creative juices to create presentation materials that are as outside the box as you are. Utilize innovative design and fresh content for handouts, slides, buttons, bumper stickers—anything that will help spread the word about your message.

3. Don't forget to include a road map that shows an overall plan for your fresh idea from start to finish. This will assure your audience that you know where you're going.

4. Don't neglect to practice in a feedback-rich environment in front of at least one critical left-brained person you can trust. He or she can help ensure that you don't come across as too high level or abstract for your audience.

5. When you are ready to debut your speech, don't send out invitations en masse. Be sure to populate your audience with like-minded people open to new ideas. They will lend an overall atmosphere of support to your delivery.

THE IDEAL CREATOR

There is no such thing as a bad persona. There are only areas to improve on within your range of strengths and weaknesses. With that in mind, what do ideal Creators look like?

1. They invest a significant amount of time researching their message, acknowledging that they have a tendency to share without becoming familiar with each angle.

2. They come equipped to each presentation with the capability to answer any questions that they may face.

3. They engage with their audience offstage, ensuring that they come across as the most knowledgeable and credible speaker on their particular topic.

What about Jeff, our enthusiastic head of marketing? If he put in the work to become an ideal Creator, his story might look like this:

1. Jeff becomes familiar with the designers' needs, and he is able to illustrate clearly how the new software could help their productivity.

2. Jeff eliminates audience doubt by filling each slide with supporting data that he's worked hard to find.

3. Because his coworkers already know that Jeff cares about the company itself, they are impressed by his thoughtful initiative, and they

are ready to take the next step rather than just promising to look into the software themselves later.

Creators in every industry inspire the world with great ideas and innovative processes that people don't even realize need an update. Their tendency toward action can achieve much while other personalities procrastinate. With just a little more thoughtful preparation in their Exploration work and a greater openness to discuss difficult questions and customize their message to a specific audience, Creators can take over the world. Don't be afraid to let that god complex shine, Creators.

Chapter 7

THE CURATOR

MEET THE CURATOR

Leopards don't stay in one place; they wander through jungles and across rivers to hunt their prey. Curators are somewhat like a leopard in this way, as their messages also travel a long distance through social media, webinars, conferences, and beyond.

A Curator's message travels far and wide. The reason this journey is such a success is careful planning and preparation. If you scored as a Curator, you are prone to selecting messages that will have long-term, long-range impact on the world. You like big-picture ideas, and you are excited about concepts that could have a positive ripple effect, even if it means that the message travels far beyond your own spotlight. You are also skilled at showing your audience a plan of what they need to do the minute they walk out of the room, and you provide plenty of resources and information to guide them.

You make a memorable impression on audiences because of all the extra work you tend to put into a presentation. Everything is well researched, well designed, and clear. You could quiz members of your audience a month from the time they heard your message, and they would remember your main points or overall purpose. Not a lot of presenters can make their words that sticky, but a Curator can.

As with all of the personas, there are areas in which a Curator can improve. Their main struggle is their onstage technique, whether because of a lack of experience or a lack of natural skill. They have a level of discomfort with conversational techniques, nonverbal behavior, and other aspects that make up their experience onstage.

Your expectations for your performance may be too high, or perhaps you feel that a strong message will be enough to make up for any awkward delivery. Either way, Curators should take a step back from their large vision, and they should assess their performance to find out where their delivery problems lie.

You can still carry the banner of a great message, even with some delivery discomfort. If the great Laurence Olivier could face his stage fright and perform Shakespeare's plays, you can learn how to refine your delivery presence and become bold. Either way, Curators always move toward their journey's end with purpose and skill.

HOW YOU SCORED

The Curator Spotlight (Video):
http://ethos3.com/treats/curator

So how did you score the Curator? These results were calculated using our four-quadrant algorithm in which anything on the outside corner of the specific quadrant is considered high and anything near the main intersection is considered mid-low (Figure 7.1). Here is a simple rundown of your placement in each quadrant and how we arrived at your profile:

EXPLORATION

Curators put in the work to make their messages memorable and meaningful, which is why they score well in this quadrant. This work includes making sure your design looks sharp or the flow of your content is logical and clear. You aren't afraid to roll up your sleeves and devote time to preparation to see that the audience gets the most from their time. The only factor that may pull your score down in this quadrant is a lack of out-loud rehearsal or other practice techniques that can strengthen your delivery.

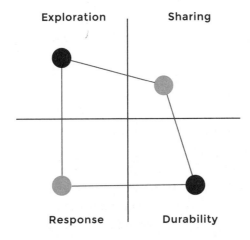

Figure 7.1 The Curator

SHARING

Curators score in the mid- to low range in this quadrant, which indicates that there is some work to be done. Maybe you've always felt that a presentation should be a formal event, for example. You put on a suit, you slick back your hair, and you deliver your message with clarity and strength. But there is more to it: audiences need to feel a connection with you to be moved by your message. You should use more updated tactics such as storytelling, nonverbal cues, and even humor to capture short attention spans today. The key word here is "authenticity." If Curators improve in this quadrant, they can become unstoppable.

RESPONSE

When your presentation ends, you're ready to devote extra time to make sure that each and every audience member's questions are answered and concerns addressed. Your desire to cater to your audience's needs is reflected in your high score for Response, which is all about networking and making a person-to-person connection. You are the ideal presenter to use interactive polls or other ways to gauge audience response, mostly because you want to ensure that your message "clicks" with everyone.

Another reason your Response score is high is that you are more comfortable talking *with* people in person than you are with talking *at* people from the stage.

DURABILITY

Curators excel in this category because of their dedication to big, earth-shaking ideas. You understand that a presentation is more than an opportunity to educate a single audience. It can be a chance to launch a platform or create converts. Your vision might be as big as the Internet itself, stretching across borders to audiences around the world. With your existing know-how in Exploration, this may well be within reach.

SPOTTING A CURATOR IN THE WILD

Meet Franklin, a sales associate at Yellow Hippo Technologies, a company with a broad catalog of small yet necessary tech gadgets, ranging from speedy phone chargers to fashionable headphones. Franklin has been working in the sales division for years, mostly talking to existing clients and managing relationships.

Franklin is incredible at his job for one key reason: he knows the company catalog inside and out. There isn't a tech spec that he's not fully versed in, not a single headphone line that he can't trace like a family tree. His bosses love how thorough and helpful he is. He's a walking sales encyclopedia.

But things are changing at Yellow Hippo Technologies. Someone needs to take the company's latest offerings on the road with a brand-new presentation. Franklin isn't experienced with in-person sales, but he is more than willing to accept the challenge and leave the comfort of the office.

The problem isn't that Franklin is inexperienced at sales or with the Yellow Hippo catalog but rather that he's an inexperienced presenter. He hasn't delivered a speech in front of an audience since his brother's wedding, and he suffers from stage fright. His palms sweat, his head mysteriously itches, and his stomach churns, and he often forgets his main points. Even though he's determined to overcome his fear and succeed on the road, he just isn't sure where to start.

One of the key struggles that Franklin and most Curators like him face is the bulk of their own knowledge. The weight of the entire Yellow Hippo Technologies catalog has made him nervous about forgetting a spec or an important fact about the line. He is using flash cards to memorize even more information, which will hurt his presentation more than it will help it.

Franklin needs to revise his entire philosophy about onstage presenting. The way he views it, presenting is more like a test that the audience grades you on. Stumbling and forgetting main points equal a lower grade, while smoothly rattling off details from the catalog equals a higher grade. Instead, it's more like guiding a conversation. Franklin needs to use his natural conversational ability to gauge what his audience wants to hear and then speak on the subject accordingly. He should determine what matters to the audience and then work to cut back his content.

Curators need to find a way to make themselves comfortable. What if Franklin started off his presentation with a Q&A session before the sales pitch even began, to uncover his audience's needs and hear their expectations? What if he told a personal story about working for Yellow Hippo Technologies to boost his credibility rather than presenting an overstuffed About Us slide? When he becomes more authentic, more conversational, and less worried about being "correct," Franklin will become a much stronger sales presenter. He also might be able to ward off some of those pesky public speaking heebie-jeebies in the process.

YOUR NATURAL HABITAT

No matter what the audience size is, no matter how big or small the room may be, presenting in front of other people makes most Curators cringe. Luckily for you, this anxiety dissipates when the talk ends and you get a chance to network with your audience. You don't mind one-on-one conversations, so utilize this skill by turning your presentation into a more interactive experience. This can include posing hypothetical questions, facilitating audience activities, and having a lengthy Q&A during your talk.

Like Franklin, you may want to create a habitat that accommodates your style. Consider moving chairs into a circle to create a round table effect, or try to find ways to start your talk with a conversation. Ask questions and give your audience time to process and answer along the way. Most will appreciate the interactive experience, and they will enjoy sharing their thoughts. Break free from what you consider a traditional presentation experience.

BRAWN (STRENGTHS)

Passionate

Inspiring

Clear

You have a natural gift for selecting ideas that deserve a presentation and crafting messages that speak to something deep inside your audience. You care about them, and this is evident in everything you do. That includes preparation before your talk as well as follow-up afterward.

Curators also succeed at making each point they deliver clear and jargon free to appeal to a wide audience. This is evident in your high score in Durability and Response. It's crucial that an audience know what next steps they can take to follow your call to action. Curators provide their listeners with a clear road map and instructions on how to get from A to B.

TRAPS (WEAKNESSES)

Uncomfortable

Routine

Unrehearsed

Curators choose their words carefully, but the way that they deliver the message is a completely different story. Whether it's a low vocal tone, stiff body language, or a general terror about being onstage, your delivery needs a little tune-up. You might spend plenty of time rehearsing, but if it's more about memorization than about finding your voice onstage, it may be hurting your presentation.

Spend just as much time working on yourself as you would working on an important message even if you feel it's unnecessary and doesn't add value. Trust us, it does, and your audience will be more willing to give you a larger share of their attention.

YOUR NATURAL ALLY

Want to learn how to strengthen your onstage presence? Take lessons from Performers (Chapter 13) and connect with the persona to see how they execute a great delivery.

YOUR PREY

Personalities who don't need or want a flashy performance will look past any delivery fumbles and appreciate your message. Other presenters who also put a lot of work into preparation, such as Scientists and Producers, will also be persuaded by your passion and breadth of knowledge. The good news for Curators is that they tend to have more willing prey than predators; you might even consider them the omnivores of the presenting world.

YOUR PREDATORS

On the other side of the coin are the ever-deadly extroverted types who love to be entertained. They can't focus on your key points unless you illustrate them with a parable, a joke, or some other memorable device. Think of how Bill Nye the Science Guy presents dry information and you'll have an idea of the kind of entertainment value your predators are hungry for.

FIVE DOS AND DON'TS

DOS

1. Share the love! Equally distribute your prep time between presentation research and onstage rehearsal to deliver a message that's as impressive as all of the behind-the-scenes work you do beforehand.

2. Rehearse your presentation from start to finish at least three to five times before you deliver it. No cheating! Make sure you are practicing proudly and out loud.

3. Get technical by incorporating the use of a digital timer while you practice to make sure that you aren't going too fast or too slow. Consider recording yourself with your phone to troubleshoot delivery errors.

4. Take a cue from famous boxers by observing and learning while you watch (rewatch and rewatch some more) your favorite speeches to gather pointers for your own delivery.

5. Use your ability to make one-on-one connections to your advantage. Schedule time after your talk for an in-depth Q&A session or even an open-ended discussion with your audience.

DON'TS

1. Don't doubt your ability to overcome stage fright and discomfort in front of an audience. Some of the best speakers throughout history have done so with plentiful practice and experience onstage.

2. Don't underestimate the power that delivery has on persuasion. Facts and stats will never have the same effect as a story, a human connection, or an emotionally driven pitch.

3. Don't forget to move around the stage and use natural hand gestures to convey excitement and passion about your subject. Formal delivery behind a lectern is a thing of the past.

4. Don't be afraid to broaden the size of your audience, especially if your message has potentially long-term and widespread effects. You can still host interactive activities such as a Q&A. Just make sure to let your audience know and prepare for it beforehand.

5. Don't neglect to add a final directive at the end of your presentation, even if it's a high-level message. Suggest a website that your audience could visit, a newsletter they could subscribe to, or something similar. You have the power to convince, so do it!

THE IDEAL CURATOR

There is no such thing as a bad persona. There are only areas to improve on within your range of strengths and weaknesses. With that in mind, what do ideal Curators look like?

1. They use creative rehearsal tactics to look and feel more natural on-stage, such as movement, posture, and storytelling techniques.

2. They refine their focus during delivery to be more authentic, not more informative.

3. They interact with their audience during their presentation, asking questions and making them feel involved at each stage.

Let's revisit the tale of Franklin, our sales team member who suffers from stage fright. What happens if he works on the Sharing quadrant to improve his skills before he hits the road to deliver the Yellow Hippo Technologies sales deck?

1. He ignores traditional presentation wisdom and discovers what will make him most comfortable before his talk: a chat over coffee with the potential client before he starts.

2. He uses a hyperlinked main menu in his presentation to talk about only the products that the clients are interested in, relieving him of the pressure to memorize.

3. He weaves in stories throughout the talk to make his pitch more personal, expressing his passion for Yellow Hippo Technologies.

Ideal Curators recognize that they struggle with delivery, and they take creative steps to improve it. Everything else works in the Curators' favor to succeed: they have a great message; the audience is clear about the Curators' main points; and they are willing to put in as much work as necessary. Like your traveling leopard mascot, your message is ready to venture long distances.

Chapter 8

THE DEMONSTRATOR

MEET THE DEMONSTRATOR

Like the beautiful peacock, you love to put your best qualities on display for an audience. You know what an audience loves to see, and you use that information to dazzle onstage. Demonstrators are known for their hard work in the preparation stage, which leads to flawless delivery. In short, when a Demonstrator steps onstage, you can expect a brilliant show.

If you scored this personality, you already know the importance of high-quality presentation materials paired with careful audience research. You are dedicated to making your message more compelling onstage, using tactics such as movement, gestures, a range of vocal tone, and more. Perhaps you were born with an innate sense that performance is important, or you may have had experience onstage in a different capacity. Either way, Demonstrators value their audience's time, and they know exactly how to use this time wisely to convey their content.

However, sometimes a beautiful display of feathers and a sassy bird dance are simply not enough to create a long-lasting impression. Demonstrators tend to spend less time working on the impact of their message after the talk is given, instead keeping their focus on delivery. All of their flash occasionally comes with a price: audiences may be too distracted by the show to remember the main points and follow up on calls to action.

As a Demonstrator, you need to work on adding a long-range view to your perspective on what should and shouldn't be in a presentation. When you offer your audience plenty of actionable next steps, they will know exactly what to do once the presentation is finished. You also may consider using some of the energy during preparation for your talk to develop a unique platform. This could entail creating a Twitter hashtag, a social media page, or a newsletter that keeps audience members informed and engaged long after the talk is finished.

Demonstrators are one of those classic pitchmen personalities: they are loud and attention grabbing, and they make people stop flipping through channels to catch the miracle of their demonstrations. However, Demonstrators need to think far beyond the one-bird show to add extra value for their audience. Let's dig a little bit deeper into what we mean.

HOW YOU SCORED

The Demonstrator Spotlight (Video):
http://ethos3.com/treats/demonstrator

So how did you score the Demonstrator? These results were calculated using our four-quadrant algorithm in which anything on the outside corner of the specific quadrant is considered high and anything near the main intersection is considered mid-low (Figure 8.1). Here is a simple rundown of your placement in each quadrant and how we arrived at your profile:

EXPLORATION

Demonstrators care about how their audience perceives them, so they tend to score in the mid- to high range of Exploration. You most likely are motivated to push yourself in this quadrant because you care about what your audience thinks of you and your message. You like to know all that you can about the people who will attend your talk, and you try to alter your style to match their preferences. If it's a corporate environment, you are happy to wear a nice jacket. If it's a more casual space, you might

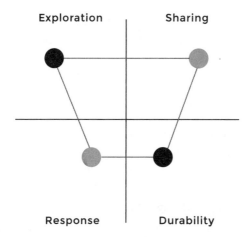

Exploration | Sharing

Response | Durability

Figure 8.1 The Demonstrator

throw in a few more jokes than normal. The only thing Demonstrators should be mindful of is how they can best prepare for the long term, beyond their time onstage (see Durability).

SHARING

Demonstrators score in the high range of the Sharing quadrant. This is because you tend to put on an electric performance, making good use of gestures, vocal tone, and movement to get your message across. You know that audiences won't pay attention unless they are entertained, and you use this knowledge to your advantage no matter what subject you speak on. This is by far your strongest quadrant, and it even reflects a knack for performance outside of the business realm.

RESPONSE

Because they put a lot of their natural talent and energy into Exploration and Sharing, Demonstrators tend to score in the mid- to low range of the Response quadrant. You might be the kind of presenter who is relieved when a talk is finished, and you feel as if the task has been checked off your list. However, great presenters never stop working when they step offstage. They use networking and other engaging techniques to keep their audiences thinking and talking about their message long after the event is over.

DURABILITY

Similar to the Response quadrant, Demonstrators score low in Durability because their focus may be limited to the event they are speaking at … and not much further beyond that. You may have never considered going global with your message, creating a website, or empowering other presenters to spread the good news. We encourage all presenters who score well in the Sharing quadrant to consider a broader platform: if you have the natural ability, why waste it?

SPOTTING A DEMONSTRATOR IN THE WILD

Meet Christine, who works for a nonprofit organization that raises money for low-income families in her city. Although most of her coworkers don't know it, she minored in theater at college, and she uses the techniques she learned to become a better speaker.

This has helped her tremendously throughout her career. She uses acting techniques such as changing her vocal tone to add emphasis, and she often rehearses casual speeches late after work in order to seem more natural. Memorizing Shakespeare plays has prepared her to remember important points when she addresses local committees, providing them with statistics that most of her team doesn't bother to learn. This potent combination has helped her organization raise thousands of dollars, and it has also elevated her from intern to strategist.

The problem that Christine faces is that each time she raises money, it only meets a short-term goal for the organization and the families it supports. She generates the bulk of funding at annual charity events, but the amount raised varies and is unreliable. She does a great job persuading donors to sign a one-time check, but she doesn't realize that it's within her power to meet long-term goals and generate regular donations.

This is where Durability comes in. Christine needs to create a platform for her message and cultivate personal relationships with her audience. This can be accomplished by something as simple as an e-mail newsletter that she sends personally, with stories about local families that the organization helps.

Christine has the vibrant energy and ability to convince her audience that they should join her on a long-term journey for the sake of local families, but she is too focused on doing a great job on an event-to-event basis. She needs to grab a hammer, some plywood, and a few nails and extend her stage in all directions. The Internet can become her stage. Networking events can become her stage. In short, anywhere she can add in a few words can become part of a much larger platform that will benefit her cause.

Demonstrators thrive in one-and-done environments, which is why they put so much energy into the short burst of a single presentation. But to become stronger, Christine needs to think bigger. To succeed, she'll need to stretch her natural ability out to venues beyond committee meetings and events. In the words of her hero Shakespeare, "All the world's a stage."

YOUR NATURAL HABITAT

You are probably already aware of where you perform best: center stage with the brightest spotlight possible. Because you are comfortable onstage no matter what the message or circumstance may be, our best recommendation is that you continue being your most authentic self and try not to let another presenter step on your toes.

Being comfortable in front of others doesn't come without a cost. The reason Demonstrators are successful under those hot spotlights is that they work so hard on preparation. Resist the temptation to cut back your rehearsal time or just wing it when you are going to deliver a familiar subject. Your dedication is your secret sauce; without it, you're serving up cold, plain oatmeal.

BRAWN (STRENGTHS)

Entertaining

Prepared

Unique

You excel at thorough preparation, especially for delivery. This usually includes rehearsing out loud, working on your script, and practicing a few stories that flow naturally into your talk. This preparation pays off by making you fascinating to watch and different from many other presenters who tend to fumble and "um" their way through a presentation.

For some presenters, poor rehearsal can lead them to stumble. Perhaps they're trying to deliver too many memorized points, or maybe their structure is too strict. Demonstrators have a keen sense of what they need to work on, so they don't waste time worrying about the order of their key messages or which opening quotes they should memorize. This natural ability to self-evaluate enables them to spend preparation time wisely, and it adds that bit of sparkle to delivery.

TRAPS (WEAKNESSES)

Breezy

Unactionable

Short term

Since Demonstrators put so much effort into their performance onstage, their message can sometimes suffer from being so light that they float away. Audiences will enjoy a flashy performance, but they won't remember the important details if serious weight is not applied to the message. Always include a call to action that the audience can tackle once you finish speaking, and ensure that the audience members are clear about what exactly that entails.

Take this a step further, and think long term. Don't just send them to a website one time. Ask them to download an app that they can interact with daily. Don't meekly offer your contact information. Sign them up for your digital newsletter the second they walk through the door. Too often, Demonstrators let a perfectly good message go to waste with a short-term mindset.

YOUR NATURAL ALLY

Want to work on Response and Durability? Connect with Advocators (Chapter 3) to improve your skills.

YOUR PREY

Demonstrators appeal to those who expect to be entertained, moved, and amused. They even have the ability to convince a few data-driven types to crack a smile during their talk. Many other profiles who enjoy the act of delivering a presentation, such as Performers and Educators, will be able to see and appreciate the hard work you did to prepare.

YOUR PREDATORS

Any personalies that expect to have their lives changed by your talk, such as Liberators or Curators, will be disappointed if you don't provide enough meat for them to gnaw on. Try to see it from your audience's perspective, and answer their question: "What's in it for me?" Your predators may also feel frustrated if you finish the presentation without giving them time for questions, networking, and other interactions. Just remember that for most audience members, a presentation doesn't end when you stop talking.

FIVE DOS AND DON'TS

DOS

1. As you prepare for your speech, ask yourself, "How can I affect my audience in a long-term way?" Keep this answer in mind as you add value to your content and thereby increase the overall value to your audience.

2. Try a group activity in your next talk. It doesn't have to be complicated. It just needs to get your audience excited about the message in a more personal way. Challenge them to reveal something to their neighbors, sketch a relevant doodle, or even share a short personal experience that ties back to your main points.

3. Always land the plane of your argument by providing the audience with two things: a recap of the points you covered and a call to action that tells them what you would like them to do after they leave the room.

4. Measure the impact of your delivery by using audience polls or surveys, or asking a friend to ascertain whether you provided a strong answer to the question, "What's in it for me?"

5. The presentation doesn't have to end when your speech is over. Make time for Q&A, networking, mingling, and other interactive activities to win over your audience even further.

DON'TS

1. Don't get lazy about your prep work. It's one of your strongest assets, and it sets you apart from the competition. Even if you're feeling comfortable with your skill set, you can always be better.

2. Don't be forgettable! Decide in the preparation phase which of your points are most important and then use design or delivery to emphasize them, repeating those points at least twice during your talk.

3. Don't spend your preparation time exclusively focused on delivery. Your message can and should live beyond the event itself. The question you should ask is, "How can I get it there?"

4. Don't limit the size of your audience. You are a memorable presenter and have the ability to create large-scale change with a huge audience and an online platform.

5. Don't underestimate your ability to persuade an audience and change minds. If you're entertaining a group but leaving them without a decision or a new piece of information, what is the point of all that hard work?

THE IDEAL DEMONSTRATOR

There is no such thing as a bad persona. There are only areas to improve on within your range of strengths and weaknesses. With that in mind, what do ideal Demonstrators look like?

1. They create long-term goals to help benefit both their audience and their message.

2. They mingle with their audience when the talk is finished, tying up loose ends and answering questions with the same cheerful energy they had during their talk.

3. They seek fresh, creative ways to make their message more durable in the future. This can include a guerrilla marketing strategy, such as starting a catchy hashtag on social media for their concept.

What happens when Christine, our theater-loving Demonstrator, improves her skills and becomes the best version of herself?

1. She develops a new plan to engage donors over the course of an entire year through marketing tactics based on her committee messages.

2. She continues to work on her performance onstage, but she is also mindful to keep this high energy going while offstage.

3. She makes sure that her audience is empowered to act, and she is very clear on how they can continue to be involved with the charity even without providing financial support.

With peacock grace, Demonstrators don't have to worry about flopping onstage. They have fully preened and prepared beforehand to deliver a message they know will sound good. The real challenge begins when the demonstration is over: How can you work on giving your message longevity? How can you make the message a part of your life and your audience's lives in the long term? With a little bit more vision and just slightly more work than you already put into Exploration, you can become the best bird in the flock.

Chapter 9

THE DIRECTOR

MEET THE DIRECTOR

When Directors walk onstage, people sit up straight in their chairs. Directors command respect, which lends credibility to their presentations, regardless of their public speaking experience.

Directors' presentations are filled with actionable items that extend far beyond the conference room. They want to see long-term change in their audience, but they will often settle for a meaningful takeaway. The word "change" is key because Directors use presentations as a means to trigger important shifts in others.

How do you recognize this breed of presenter in the wild? If the speaker is asking you to go out into the world and get something done, you're probably in the presence of a Director.

If you received this profile, there are some positive traits we can conclude about your personality type outside of the conference room. If there's a fire to be extinguished, you're there with a hose. If a friend needs support, you're there with a hug and some cake. In a leadership role, you stay calm under pressure, and most important, you are able to deliver assertive yet empathetic messages.

Because of your level-headedness, audiences tend to trust your decisive authority, and they will continue to respect it even if you have bad news to share. People want to be led, and you're the leader of the pack.

However, Directors also need to be wary of asking too much of their audiences or setting their expectations of themselves and others too high.

HOW YOU SCORED

The Director Spotlight (Video):
http://ethos3.com/treats/director

So how did you score the Director? These results were calculated using our four-quadrant algorithm in which anything on the outside corner of the specific quadrant is considered high and anything near the main intersection is considered mid-low (Figure 9.1). Here is a simple rundown of your placement in each quadrant and how we arrived at your profile:

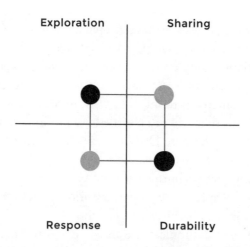

Figure 9.1 The Director

EXPLORATION

Directors tend to spend a moderate amount of time working in this area, relying instead on their own experience and the research they put into the task. You probably scored in the mid- to low range of the quadrant because you may not believe that learning a new design skill or writing, and rewriting, scripts is necessary. You may want a presentation to look good, but you won't obsess over something with a short shelf life. Perhaps you feel uncomfortable and unsure of where to start when it comes to preparation. Either way, this is definitely an area to work on.

SHARING

Directors are a moderate, middle-of-the-road kind of personality, so they tend to score in the mid- to low range of the quadrant. You come across as clear and knowledgeable, but you may lack a vibrant energy that comes with more experienced (and perhaps extroverted) presenters. You'll want to work on adding that energy to your performance through multiple rehearsals or other techniques to get you more engaged with delivery. Refer to Chapter 20 for helpful tips on delivery.

RESPONSE

Directors put the right amount of energy into the after-presentation work. You are comfortable answering any questions, but you respect that people may be busy or have other worries. Again, you scored in the middle area of this quadrant. If you feel like you're seeing a pattern here, you are. Directors are so well rounded that they look like a doughnut if you squint.

DURABILITY

Directors can deliver talks that have long-lasting impact, but most deal with immediate concerns that need to be addressed. Your score placed you in the mid- to low range (surprise!) of Durability. Improving your score in this area requires you to ask a little more of your content. What are the long-term benefits for your audience? How can you spread the word even further? Those are the kinds of changes that Durability requires.

SPOTTING A DIRECTOR IN THE WILD

Meet Mark, a go-getter with limited presentation skills, part of a startup team that has created an app that provides users with a smarter, shareable to-do list called ZipeeSpread. They will be presenting ZipeeSpread to their first round of investors. Mark has a background in business development, so he was picked to deliver the first few presentations. He feels passionately about this project, and he knows the app will have broad appeal. His friends and family have been generous with pats on the back and encouragement.

But here is the problem: Mark feels like he has enough enthusiasm to stand in front of investors and deliver a successful pitch. Even though he's inexperienced, he feels that the product and his bright smile will make him successful. When asked if he is prepared, if he is capable of delivery, and if he has a strong long-term message, his answers would be *yes, yes,* and *a big fat YES!* It's great for Mark to feel good about what he has to offer, but none of that will help him stand out from other pitches.

Now let's examine why he's probably about to waste 15 minutes of an investor's time. The first aspect is Mark's level of preparation. His PowerPoint looks dated, and he hasn't done a ton of research about competitive apps in the market. A quick Google search should suffice, right? Probably not. Technology is changing; audiences are smarter. He is going to have to put in the hard work and learn some new skills in order to impress. Hiring a professional designer for his materials, subscribing to industry publications and magazines, and refining his content are all ways he can improve.

What about his delivery? While he benefits from a winning smile, Mark puts a lot of faith in his social ability. A great pitch results from practicing in front of the mirror over and over again. A strong delivery is one that has been tweaked, rehearsed, cried over, and rehearsed again. He's going to have to move far past the idea of being naturally gifted and realize that all naturals still have to put in some time.

Classic Directors do the amount of work that they *assume* is necessary. They trust the level of knowledge they have going into a project, and the same is true for design and delivery. But this puts them squarely in the range of just-OK work. If they were being graded for each aspect of their presentation, they would get a lot of C+ and B- grades.

It's not about using what you already know. It's about putting in the extra work because your audience can tell the difference in quality. Mark is going to have to spend more time than he's used to on this project, and he needs to not listen to all his well-meaning friends who say that he's ready to make millions.

Directors need to realize two things: that their existing skill set isn't enough to impress and that they have it within themselves to strengthen their style considerably. Give Mark a handful more days of prep time, a peek at the intensity of his competition, and fewer friends telling him that he's the best. The end result? A totally new, much more prepared, much more down-to-business Mark.

YOUR NATURAL HABITAT

A natural habitat describes the place you feel most comfortable delivering your message, usually in relation to the size of the audience and the formality of the event. For Directors, the best habitat is one in which a decision needs to be made because they are there to deliver the deciding presentation. You are most comfortable in boardrooms, conference rooms, and other places where the stakes are high and a voice of reason is required. You also tend to perform best when you're invested in the other participants or audience members' lives, which makes you a strong internal company presenter.

Directors offer a balanced voice in an unbalanced room. They are like the reasonable politician who says, "See here!" in the middle of a shouting battle between two opposing sides. This gives you a solid advantage when hosting a Q&A session or any other opportunity to hold a discussion with your audience. Embrace and appreciate this skill!

BRAWN (STRENGTHS)

Decisiveness

Fairness

Integrity

You are steered evenly by a strong moral compass, which serves as the basis for all of your messaging and presentations. This gives you a reputation for trustworthiness and fairness, like an Old Faithful of good advice. You also care a great deal about your audience, and you want to make sure their needs are fully addressed. This makes you an endearing personality even if you aren't putting in a lot of extra work to leave them fully entertained by the end of the speech.

Consistency is also your strength, as your personality both onstage and off reflects the same values and style. Make up for any presenting weaknesses by hosting an in-depth discussion at the end of the talk. Use that time to clarify questions and prove that you are an authority in your field.

TRAPS (WEAKNESSES)

Condescending

Dull

Controlling

Because doling out advice is second nature to you, you risk alienating members of your audience who feel that they are being talked down to. Your ability to step easily into new situations can bring out a tendency to control, which may be unwelcome if they weren't looking for a new leader. And finally, all of the grandfatherly wisdom you have stored up can equate to a boring presentation if not supported by some personality.

All of these weaknesses are amplified when you don't take time to prepare or when you're content with your current skill level. Listen to feedback. Give yourself more aggressive goals. In short, stop being comfortable! Get off that comfy couch of past experience.

YOUR NATURAL ALLY

Want to learn how to improve your skills and become stronger in each quadrant? Take lessons from Liberators (Chapter 11) and connect in real life to see them in their natural habitat.

YOUR PREY

Fortunately for most Directors, people love to be told what to do. Indecisiveness plagues both the professional and personal arenas, which is where you provide value by sharing the advice and guidance they need. Most audience members appreciate your level-headedness and straightforward style, and they will be especially receptive to your message if they know you offstage. In short, you appeal to those who like to sit in the front row of a classroom, who are already prepped and ready to take notes.

YOUR PREDATORS

Other Directors, skeptics, rule breakers, and risk takers will be hesitant to listen to your guidance and quietly accept your leadership. You may need to add proof such as stats and facts to support your seasoned advice and boost your credibility in front of these doubters. Skeptics tend to become bored quickly. Your message should be credible, with enough fun thrown in to capture their full attention.

FIVE DOS AND DON'TS

DOS

1. Liven up your presentation by including at least one to three personal stories. These can be used to warm up your introduction, illustrate a main point in the middle, or bring the talk to a close.

2. If you offer a piece of advice, suggestion, or key idea, then be sure to back it up with an anecdote from your own experience or a credible data point to establish yourself as an authority.

3. Since you are prone to giving advice, make sure that your talk has only one takeaway for the audience to act on later. Make this call to action clear by prefacing it with a statement like, "If you leave here with only one thing . . ."

4. Ask a friend to watch you rehearse your presentation and rate you on one main area: how tired were they by the end of your speech? Work on keeping them energized by including interactive questions, unexpected props, or attention-grabbing slides.

5. Make sure your call to action is something you, your friends, and even your family would want to jump up and accomplish once the talk is over.

DON'TS

1. Don't neglect to address your audience's needs immediately in the presentation to establish that you care and are empathetic about the worries that keep them up at night.

2. Don't forget to include media-rich supporting elements as part of your presentation to enhance your talk. These can include unique handouts, well-designed great slides, props, and other aids to help make your message more memorable.

3. Don't use a condescending tone, and cut out questions such as, "Does that make sense?" or "Do you understand?" If you're not sure if you use these expressions, film and watch yourself during a rehearsal session or ask a friend.

4. Don't hesitate to include a lengthy Q&A at the end of your presentation: your strength is in guiding others, and you will establish credibility through this exchange.

5. Work on keeping your delivery style more natural with multiple practice sessions, never memorization.

THE IDEAL DIRECTOR

There is no such thing as a bad persona. There are only areas to improve on within your range of strengths and weaknesses. With that in mind, what do ideal Directors look like?

1. They are able to use inspiration and encouragement to lead their audience toward actionable goals that will have a positive influence.

2. They are credible, inviting speakers who know how to establish themselves as an authority in their field.

3. No matter the circumstance, their words make each audience member feel valued and important.

Let's revisit Mark, member of a startup team, who until now felt confident enough to deliver a pitch about ZipeeSpread without a ton of prep work. He is now switching gears and following our tips, and here is how his revised presentation goes:

1. He spends time researching the current market, and he throws in stats and facts, which add meaningful weight to his talk.

2. He rehearses his presentation eight different times in front of a mirror, perfecting his performance and appearing much more credible.

3. He provides his audience with a way to connect with him after the talk, giving him the information he needs to follow up on his pitch and close the deal.

Natural leaders often make strong, persuasive speakers. But ideal Directors have something more than just natural leadership. They also have a great deal of empathy for their audience, which means that they want to see personal change in the lives of their listeners. They are altruistic and add value for the greater good rather than being merely informative or impressive. In short, they care.

Chapter 10

THE EDUCATOR

MEET THE EDUCATOR

Educators are represented by the strong elephant, which tradition-ally signifies intelligence and an imposing demeanor. This is be-cause Educators put a lot of hard work into the preparation of their message, and they are imposing figures onstage with their authoritative style. They impress their audience with their wit as well as their scope of knowledge, making them thorough presenters who know the task at hand and crush expectations beneath their jumbo-size elephant feet.

When Educators walk onstage, they convey that they're in charge through nonverbal cues. They state their main points plainly, and they take care to explain any unfamiliar vocabulary or jargon that the audi-ence may encounter. If members of their audience have questions, they are fully capable of handling even the most uncomfortable or off-the-wall inquiry. Organized, powerful, and clear—that's the Educator style.

If you received this profile, you already have everything you need to become a solid presenter. This could be due to past experience, but it may also be because you are dedicated and single-minded when it comes to challenges in business and in your personal life. You scored well in the quadrants in which a thorough knowledge of your audience and subject matter is required, and this is also reflected in your natural range.

The only foe that Educators face is the longevity of their message. This may be because the content you deliver is itself limited. Maybe you're a math teacher who shares the building blocks only to the next lesson, or perhaps you are a salesperson specializing in one-time purchases of big-ticket items, such as air-conditioning units. It can be hard to see how your subject matter could be used on a bigger platform or how it could change the world. Perhaps you struggle with the fact that your words have immediate value only for your audience.

But there is good news! Educators can always adapt. What if you found ways to become a part of your audience's life, even if your message is short term? What if you created a platform for your single-use product, becoming the expert in your niche market? With a little bit of vision, your persona can become the ruler of the savannah.

HOW YOU SCORED

The Educator Spotlight (Video):
http://ethos3.com/treats/educator

So how did you score the Educator? These results were calculated using our four-quadrant algorithm in which anything on the outside corner of the specific quadrant is considered high and anything near the main intersection is considered mid-low (Figure 10.1). Here is a simple rundown of your placement in each quadrant and how we arrived at your profile:

EXPLORATION

When you hear words such as "preparation," "additional materials," and "rehearsing," a bell most likely goes off in your head. Educators score on the high end of this quadrant because they know what it takes to prepare for a talk. You're not afraid to put in the extra work and long hours to edit your presentation, create good-looking slides, and work through your content until it feels just right. However, getting ready for a talk is

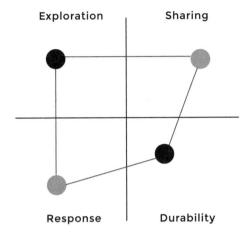

Figure 10.1 The Educator

more than just a formula that you repeat over and over again. Sometimes a pinch of creativity can help break you out of a low Durability score (see below) and give your normal talk a boost of long-term memorability.

SHARING

Educators score well in this quadrant, and we suspect it's because of all of that wonderful prep work. Even if you still suffer from a few pre-speech jitters, your audience doesn't intimidate you enough for you to make mistakes or lose sight of your ultimate goal. Educators are skilled at using examples, nonverbal cues, and even a dash of humor to keep audiences engaged and yes, even awake. For most presenters, the "awake" part is especially difficult.

RESPONSE

Because Educators often live in a world of short-term messages and long discussions, they score well in the Response quadrant. You might already have seen the benefit of group activities and Q&As throughout your career, and you know how helpful they can be in personalizing your message for different learners. Educators often come equipped with the observational skills to help them gauge audience response and act accordingly. Think of teachers who want to help their students pass the SATs. They hope that some of the larger concepts are remembered, but in general, they do a great job ensuring that the short-term formulas and facts stick for the time being.

DURABILITY

This is the only quadrant in which Educators score in the mid- to low range. Is it because you are limited by short-term messages? Or is it because you haven't considered creating a larger platform for yourself and your message? Either way, the long-term value and the length of time your message is relevant are questionable. Going back to that teacher comparison, consider the limitation of a lesson that is remembered only until the test. In this case, they may find creative ways to tie specific parts of the lesson to their students' lives, or they may perhaps build a platform for themselves that helps their message grow outside of the classroom.

SPOTTING AN EDUCATOR IN THE WILD

Meet Shelly, a Renaissance history professor at a local community college. She's been teaching for 10 years and loves her job, driven by a passion for all things Renaissance. With each new class of students, she can't wait to share her excitement and play an entire album of period-appropriate harp music.

Shelly is a realist and knows that many of her students are attending her class for credit, not necessarily because they love the Renaissance. But with each new student, she hopes to instill a bit of excitement that will carry on throughout the rest of his or her life. Since her town hosts a Renaissance fair each year, Shelly would love to see former students participate in costume and indulge in giant turkey legs.

Everyone's favorite history teacher faces a few challenges. The test format at the community college is rigorous, so her students need to remember a lot of facts and dates rather than just enjoying the literature and her engaging storytelling. She also knows that most people would rather be in creative writing workshops or at lunch, in spite of her best efforts. Sometimes a long list of kings and queens puts students to sleep faster than a lullaby played on a lute.

How can this Educator improve her own speaking style in order for her message to achieve longevity? Will she ever be able to convince her students to wear corsets and stockings to a Renaissance fair?

To be a success, Shelly needs to examine her prep work and some of the larger issues surrounding her course. If she usually teaches the Renaissance class in the winter semester but the fair is in early summer, she might consider switching the course to the spring. This way, the reward for passing the tests can be a group trip to the fair itself. She may also work on ways to make the course more interactive in general, with activities meant to simulate the Renaissance experience, such as a cooking class. Her work will take place in Exploration, which will in turn help her score in Durability.

The more she considers long-term benefits, the easier it will be for her to develop lessons and activities that will stick for her students. Shelly can feel inspired by this new perspective, thinking of her class as a Renaissance experience rather than just a few history credits for her students. Even if some of her audience will forget everything on the first day of summer break, not all of them will. Shelly can feel confident that she is putting in the work to become a more memorable speaker.

An ideal Educator doesn't have to be discouraged by a less-than-ideal message. There is always a fresh way to make the topic not only more interesting to speak about but also much more fun and memorable to the audience. Think of the best class you've ever had in your life: how did that particular Educator stand out?

YOUR NATURAL HABITAT

Educators are comfortable taking the stage in most environments, from a classroom to a large conference room and beyond. But perhaps the place they are most comfortable is in a small group setting, which allows Educators to show off their knack for group activities and discussion.

While you may prefer a smaller crowd of people looking to be educated on a particular topic, you have the ability and drive to present to a concert hall filled with people. Don't underestimate the number of people who would be interested in and engaged by your message. Consider some habitats that may be a little outside of your comfort zone, such as a podcast or a webinar for remote learners.

BRAWN (STRENGTHS)

Skillful

Effective

Dedicated

Educators don't have to be told how to present; they have enough experience and passion for their subject matter to do an excellent job on their own. Even in their personal lives, they approach tasks mindfully and with their full energy. This is indicated by their high score in Exploration, which indicates a great dose of dedication right from the start.

Your score also indicates that you are familiar with important preparation techniques such as storyboarding your content, rehearsing out loud, and restricting your on-slide text to the information that matters. Because of this, you come across as a knowledgeable presenter who won't waste your audience's time.

TRAPS (WEAKNESSES)

Limited

Changeable

Tedious

Because they are typically asked to provide educational or professional content, Educators often limit themselves with the notion that they are not able to expand to a longer-term message. If you have the ability, you should use it. Consider broadening your skills by speaking about a topic you love in a venue outside of work.

Educators also risk overwhelming their audience with too much information, especially if it's short term and not high level. Be sure you always tie your message to a big-picture takeaway for your audience so that their memory of your message will persist.

YOUR NATURAL ALLY

Want to learn ways to improve Durability? Take a lesson from Soldiers (Chapter 17) and observe how they develop long-lasting messages for their audience.

YOUR PREY

Students, lifelong learners, and those who are curious to uncover something new will love your presentation style. Anyone who also recognizes the thorough work you put into research will be impressed. You will appeal to most introverts because you deliver messages that require deeper thought to unpack. You also appeal to most extroverts because of your keen ability to manage participation activities that offer them value.

YOUR PREDATORS

Some people approach a presentation or talk with a "What's in it for me?" mindset. Make sure to demonstrate how the subject you're explaining directly relates to their day-to-day lives. You have the natural speaking ability to win them over.

FIVE DOS AND DON'TS

DOS

1. Approach your message with a lens toward the long term. How can your message affect your audience a month after your talk? How

about a year? Aim to stretch its value and give your audience something more weighty.

2. The most crucial question for Educators to ask themselves is, "How does my message benefit my audience?" A presentation doesn't have to be merely informative. It can serve a dual purpose as a catalyst to change hearts and minds.

3. Use storytelling to demonstrate how your main points fit into the lives of your audience members.

4. When your talk is finished, always provide the audience with clear next steps to experience fully the benefit of your message.

5. Have you ever considered expanding your platform? Your style would be well served by supplemental ways to spread the word, such as social media, webinars, and regular blogging.

DON'TS

1. Don't guess what your audience would like to hear or should hear. Put in the time during the research phase to learn more about their needs.

2. Don't underestimate the value of originality. Even if you must deliver a message that's conservative, adding fresh design elements and unexpected content can boost its memorability.

3. Don't overwhelm your audience with a lot of information and then leave them with a vague call to action that sounds like, "Remember all of that." Edit your main points to a much more digestible level.

4. Don't forget to empower your audience with the information, motivation, and inspiration they need to take your key concepts with them out into the world.

5. Don't avoid technology. Use social media, new design software, and digital sharing to help your message reach more people. They don't bite!

THE IDEAL EDUCATOR

There is no such thing as a bad persona. There are only areas to improve on within your range of strengths and weaknesses. With that in mind, what do ideal Educators look like?

1. They look beyond the limitation of their content, and they come up with creative methods to help extend its longevity with continued contact with their audience.

2. They realize the importance of revving up excitement with their audience, and they find fresh ways to do so with props, visual media, and meaningful interactive activities.

3. They use their preparation time not merely to rehearse and research their message but also to develop a platform for themselves as a presenter, which will last beyond the talk.

Let's revisit the tale of Shelly, our Renaissance-loving teacher who wants to instill a passion for that era within her students. What happens when she follows our tips and thinks outside the box? Here's what she tackles:

1. She shifts her goal beyond the date when the course ends, moving the semester in which it is taught to the semester in which the Renaissance fair is actually held, thereby encouraging her students' participation in the fair.

2. She uses real-life activities such as bread making and weaving to get her students physically involved with the course material.

3. She starts her own Renaissance podcast to reach history buffs around the world, beyond her small community college.

Sometimes, all it takes for an Educator to become his or her ideal self is a new perspective. Step back from the message that you need to deliver and look around. Is there a way to give yourself longevity as a presenter even if your message lasts only for a short while? How do you turn your short-term message into a much more durable, long-lasting topic? As a mighty elephant, you are an incredibly prepared and confident presenter. You have the strength to become an ideal Educator.

Chapter 11

THE LIBERATOR

MEET THE LIBERATOR

You are the architect of cloud castles: an optimistic visionary who loves to inspire. When Liberators step onstage, they share ideas that warm hearts and motivate anyone who listens. This is in part due to their natural ability and in part due to their experience in leadership and emboldening others. Either way, Liberators receive an overall strong score from the assessment because of an ideal combination of experience and personality.

The Liberator persona is represented by a lion because of the way his or her message "roars." They choose topics that have long-term value for their audience, and their messages are capable of being heard and appreciated by people with different backgrounds and perspectives. Big, loud, bold: lions are the king of their turf for a reason.

A lion's teeth aren't just for show. Liberators have the intelligence to back up their presentation with sound practical advice. Their work in the research phase ensures that they can answer tough questions with facts, stats, and examples that will support their assertions. All of that backend work not only gives them credibility as presenters but also gives them the confidence they need to deliver with power.

If you scored as a Liberator, you most likely enjoy sharing ideas that will benefit the audience in a deeper way. If you deliver a sales presentation, for instance, your focus is on creating a lengthy relationship with the client rather than just making a one-time sale. If you are a teacher, your emphasis is on the real-world application of the message far beyond the classroom. Even if speaking is not part of your daily routine, you will still find the best way to create positive change within your audience when challenged to present. This empathetic perspective helps shape the way you develop content and deliver your ideas, and it shows no matter what the topic.

Of course, it's not always about cloud castles and sunshine. Liberators can often be their own worst enemy because of overconfidence in their ability or in the message that they want to deliver. Sometimes they are so focused on the bigger picture or their platform that they forget to help audience members who need more time, more explanation, and more facts. When your eyes are focused in the distance and on the horizon, it's easy to stumble over the rocks in your path.

Ideal Liberators will be able to balance their big-picture visions with practicality, making it easy for audience members to act on what they've said. With some mindful work and a little extra effort, the lion's roar could be heard the wide world over.

HOW YOU SCORED

The Liberator Spotlight (Video):
http://ethos3.com/treats/liberator

So how did you score the Liberator? These results were calculated using our four-quadrant algorithm in which anything on the outside corner of the specific quadrant is considered high and anything near the main intersection is considered mid-low (Figure 11.1). Here is a simple rundown of your placement in each quadrant and how we arrived at your profile:

EXPLORATION

Liberators score especially well in this quadrant, and the extra work they put into preparation influences their entire speech. Your answers indicate

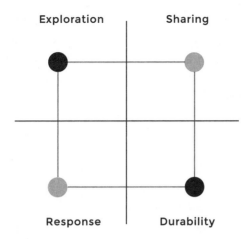

Figure 11.1 The Liberators

that you value great design, use techniques such as content storyboarding, and spend time rehearsing your presentation aloud. Much of Exploration is common sense and practical public speaking wisdom, but the bulk of your score is probably due to the passion you have for the subject. If you enjoy something, you want to make sure that others enjoy it too, which you achieve by exuding energy and coming across as a professional.

SHARING

Liberators are great at clearly and passionately sharing their message. You are energized by delivering a great speech, and you are comfortable using techniques such as storytelling and humor to enhance the overall message. If anything, the best way that Liberators can improve in this category is to make sure they are not just delivering the kind of message that they would like but delivering the kind of message that their audience will enjoy as well. To accomplish this, you might consider customizing your content in different parts to each kind of learning style (visual, auditory, reading and writing, and kinesthetic) the audience members may have.

RESPONSE

Your score fell within the mid- to high range of this quadrant, which suggests a natural strength at networking and after-presentation activities.

However, we recommend that Liberators take a closer look in this category and ask for objective feedback after a presentation. Sometimes the rush you experience after presenting may obscure how the audience really feels about your message. You may believe that you answered everyone's questions and the energy was good, but that belief could simply be a projection of your own vivacity.

DURABILITY

Your personal drive is fueled by messages that have meaning and last for a long time. Even if you haven't delivered a message or created a platform big enough to suit you, you have dreams of doing so or you are already working on it. Liberators are the ideal persona for creating, developing, and delivering messages that can change the world and stick. If you haven't started working on your long-term platform yet, what are you waiting for?

SPOTTING A LIBERATOR IN THE WILD

Meet Zoey, a full-time hospital nurse and single mother. She has been an inventor, a tinkerer, and a dreamer her whole life. She aspires to write an inspirational book for mothers who work, based on her own experiences. But it will be more than just a book: she would love to create an entire network of resources for working moms. This could include a website, an app, and a speaking tour for herself that would take her across the country. Zoey even envisions this platform to include TV—and her own talk show.

If it sounds like a pie-in-the-sky dream, it is. But what separates Zoey from other dreamers is a personal drive and a vibrant personality. When she talks, people listen. When she describes her plan for her platform, people believe that she will achieve her goals.

She has also put in the time necessary to put her plan into action. When her day job ends, her research and writing begin. She finds source data, collects true stories from other moms, and works on her book, and she is developing a presentation that she can deliver as a general overview of her platform. No stone is left unturned; her house is starting to look like a messy library of books, printed papers, folders, and bright sticky notes.

If it sounds like Zoey is on her way to becoming a great speaker ... she is. The only thing that stands in her way is her own single-mindedness. She is crafting her message for other Zoeys like her in the world, but not necessarily for a variety of audience members and different kinds of moms. To refine her message, she will need to ask a friend to listen to her pitch and make suggestions. And as difficult as it may seem, she must take those comments to heart, even if it means toning herself down onstage.

The last thing that Zoey wants is to come across as self-interested and self-focused. If her platform is truly about helping others, then she needs to better understand people who may not be Liberators like her. Not all moms share her energy or even her learning style. With a broader view, she will be better able to cater to a wider audience and guarantee the success of her efforts.

Think of her platform as a perfect ice cream sundae. No matter how delicious the elements are together, someone will always have a favorite flavor. To succeed, Zoey needs to make sure there is a scoop of everything, and that will require a little bit more work and some helpful feedback from those she trusts.

YOUR NATURAL HABITAT

Imagine this: a small coffee shop with 15 chairs lined up facing a stage. People are wandering in and out for their lattes, ignoring the performance that's about to occur. Eventually, three or four people fill the seats and wait for the speech to begin. For a Liberator, this is a horror story.

The reason this sounds so scary is that your messages are aimed at the masses, and your ideal presentation platform would reach the largest audience possible. You have jumbo-size dreams of ballroom gigs, spots on television, even the famed TED stage. These are the best places for your ideas to thrive because they are high level and broad enough to share with a wide range of people. The bigger, the better.

BRAWN (STRENGTHS)

Persuasive

Enthusiastic

Articulate

Your ability to plan far into the future gives you an advantage over more reactive presenters, and it also makes you a strong contender for thought leadership. You approach all of your projects with high energy and a go-getter attitude that audiences love to see. This is enhanced by your natural speaking skill onstage, which engages your audience with tactics used by entertainers of all backgrounds and abilities.

But it's more than entertainment: your energy is backed by the necessary research and intelligent planning required to be credible. That extra work is apparent to your audience even if they don't necessarily agree with the message itself.

TRAPS (WEAKNESSES)

Redundant

Fluffy

Self-focused

No speaker is perfect, not even a Liberator. Your presentations risk being too lofty and insubstantial if careful data is not selected to support the core points. Because feel-good messages are popular, you risk sounding like everyone else unless you offer something fresh. These actions can add up to one fluffy, forgettable message if you aren't careful.

Liberators can be prone to creating an uplifting message that they want to hear themselves rather than homing in on their audience's needs and wants. For Zoey, improving her message requires a careful understanding of what her ideal audience desires to hear.

YOUR NATURAL ALLY

Want to learn how to balance your strengths and become more approachable and down-to-earth? Take some time to learn from Directors (Chapter 9) and gain some insight by interacting with them.

YOUR PREY

Those in search of a little inspiration will be your ideal audience. The same goes for people looking for some leadership, who don't want to feel as if they are being forcefully managed into bettering themselves. High-level messages are perfect to meet these needs, especially in the hands of a capable and experienced presenter.

YOUR PREDATORS

Not everyone likes to see a half-hour sitcom end with all the loose ends tied up and a smiling family. Scholar personalities will be hesitant to accept your large-scale vision if it relies on a lot of ifs and if it is light on proof. You will need to make sure that if you teach a lesson or offer a step-by-step call to action, you consider different learning types. Some may need a demonstration, some a text-based handout, and others a hands-on group activity to feel like they fully understand your message. In general, be mindful of those who learn and understand the world differently than you do.

FIVE DOS AND DON'TS

DOS

1. Do your research before presenting a brilliant new idea to the masses: be sure to Google all avenues to see if an idea like yours already exists. If it does, then acknowledge the similarity during your speech and be very clear about your differentiation.

2. To confirm that the content of your message isn't too niche to apply to your audience, compile a list of five very different friends, relatives, and coworkers. How could your idea apply to each of them? Does it work for everyone? Build your speech to touch on the various ways your idea can be applied.

3. You're naturally the master of feel-good messages, but be sure that these big-picture ideals can have real outcomes that are reflected in your content outline.

4. Create a call to action that is clear and direct and that can be feasibly accomplished by your audience when the speech is over.

5. Let your natural enthusiasm take over when you deliver: drop the notion that you are required to come across as corporate or stiff in front of your audience. This can be achieved by rehearsing, never memorizing, your main points.

DON'TS

1. Don't let your excitement about the topic let you drop the ball on strong research, facts that can back up your main ideas, and any other supporting data that will help give your message credibility.

2. Don't make it all about you. If you are including stories in your presentation, consider using a protagonist other than you who could also benefit from your message.

3. Don't just tell your audience how great the future would be if your vision came to life. Present a complete road map of how it can be practically implemented in a timely way.

4. Don't let your ego get in the way of a great message. Accomplish this by rehearsing your presentation in front of others who are willing to tell you when they feel disconnected from your message.

5. When you come across any doubtful audience members, don't shy away from offering a Q&A session that can address their reasonable questions.

THE IDEAL LIBERATOR

There is no such thing as a bad persona. There are only areas to improve on within your range of strengths and weaknesses. With that in mind, what do ideal Liberators look like?

1. They put in the extra work to better understand their audience's needs, and they craft their message to fit different learning styles.

2. They are careful to avoid a fluffy, feel-good message that is light on proof.

3. They look beyond themselves and their own ambition to understand the world around them, and they ask for feedback even if it's unpleasant to hear.

What about the story of Zoey, our hardworking mom who dreams of creating a helpful resource for other moms in her situation? Here's how her story changes when she works to become a more ideal persona:

1. She doesn't just use Google to find the real-life stories of other moms and how they handle a busy schedule in their own way. She also interviews moms, takes notes, and incorporates their stories into the fabric of her brand.

2. She acknowledges that not everyone is like her, and she works to customize a call to action specific to different needs and personalities.

3. She presents her message to her sister and a few close friends, taking careful note of their feedback and making the necessary changes.

Lions are fierce; so are Liberators. Since you've already received a score that reflects a strong understanding of what it takes to be a great presenter, all you need to do to become ideal is work on self-awareness. If your close friends watched you present, would they say you were a perfect speaker? Find out where your blind spots are and don't let pride or confidence stop you from making the requisite changes and hearing news you might not want to hear. The end result will be a confident presentation that roars—one that's heard around the world.

Chapter 12

THE NAVIGATOR

MEET THE NAVIGATOR

P icture majestic sea turtles. They have an instinctive sense of direction, traveling on the tide from one place to another. They know exactly what they must do and how to accomplish it. If you received the Navigator persona, a similar journey takes place when you are assigned a presentation or speaking task. You have a set of internal instructions that tell you how much you should prepare and the kind of content that your audience will expect to see.

A Navigator's strongest asset is survival. You want to accomplish your task without any major missteps. Even if you lack experience, you are willing to work hard to present in front of your audience without forgetting any important points, stumbling over your words, or seeming unprepared.

Because of this, Navigators spend a lot of time in the preparation phase. They are the kinds of presenters who tinker with their slides over and over before they feel comfortable putting them in front of an audience. And even on the day of the event, they are still thinking of things they'd like to change. Much of this stems from an inherent interest in the audience's needs, hopes, concerns, likes, and dislikes. You are keenly aware of what it takes to deliver a great presentation, and you want to make sure that the audience sees what it expects.

This level of empathy and understanding also informs the way Navigators interact with their audience once the speech is finished. They are natural moderators for discussion and great at answering questions because of their preparedness. You may find that you prefer interacting with your audience more than being onstage in front of them, which you can use to your advantage by incorporating prepared group activities.

There are only two areas that can sweep Navigators out to sea: their onstage delivery style and their long-term memorability. Strong preparation doesn't always indicate a natural onstage style, and too much worry can cause discomfort. You may find that you struggle with stage fright or general anxiety in front of others, either from a lack of experience or from that accursed fight-or-flight instinct. As for long-term memorability, you may not be familiar with all of the ways a presentation can be used in the future, or you might not be aware of how to create a personal platform for yourself and your message.

Either way, Navigators tend to be well-rounded personalities who are more than capable of improving their natural skills. Sometimes it's about more than just survival. Sometimes even a familiar journey can be traveled with a little flair.

HOW YOU SCORED

The Navigator Spotlight (Video):
http://ethos3.com/treats/navigator

So how did you score the Navigator? These results were calculated using our four-quadrant algorithm in which anything on the outside corner of the specific quadrant is considered high and anything near the main intersection is considered mid-low (Figure 12.1). Here is a simple rundown of your placement in each quadrant and how we arrived at your profile:

EXPLORATION

Navigators shine brightly in this quadrant, scoring in the mid- to high range. From developing the right order of your message to making sure the design elements show up clearly on a full screen, you care about the

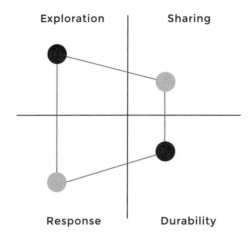

Exploration | Sharing

Response | Durability

Figure 12.1 The Navigators

details that make a presentation worth watching. You tend to listen to conventional wisdom about how many times to rehearse and what your audience expects to hear, following this tradition rather than winging it or experimenting. For most Navigators, Exploration is about making sure all of the most important boxes are checked on the preparation clipboard.

SHARING

Perhaps because of a general feeling of "eek," Navigators score in the mid- to low range of Sharing. You might not be comfortable with sharing long stories or telling jokes, perhaps because of your expectations of corporate or formal presentations. We encourage you to turn to TED, not your boss's annual sales review, for inspiration in this quadrant. This might take a bit of reverse learning: forget the formal expectations of a speech and embrace the fact that storytelling and more natural speaking styles tend to be more memorable and engaging.

RESPONSE

Navigators score well in Response. It may feel strange to them to be on-stage, and interacting with others and networking is more in line with their strengths. You are comfortable talking about the topic that you spent so long researching, and you may even feel gratified to get a little feedback after spending time in front of the group. This quadrant is where you are the most confident and clear, and it is where your audience feels the most impressed.

DURABILITY

Have you ever considered the long-term impact of your message? Have you thought of ways that it can be uploaded to social media or shared beyond the stage? Since Navigators score in the mid- to low range of Durability, your answer is most likely, "Eh." You can improve your score once you understand the cyclical nature of content, such as the classic logo for recycling. Concepts you use during a talk can be used for other messages, circling and growing and thus becoming something new. Durability is what makes that happen, paired with a long-term goal or vision.

SPOTTING A NAVIGATOR IN THE WILD

Meet Aaron, a coding pro at Note-EO, a website that acts as a digital folder to organize loose notes and lists. Each quarter, a member from the development team delivers a presentation about the challenges and successes they encountered during that time. Aaron is next to deliver a presentation, and he's freaking out about it.

Even in school, he rarely delivered a presentation outside of a few group activities. He's a likable member of the team, but he knows that it won't be enough to come across as confident and credible when his knees are shaking onstage. Aaron is the kind of guy who avoids karaoke and prays none of his friends get married so that he will have to deliver a best man speech.

In the face of these fears, Aaron is determined to do a good job. He works hard to create a clean-looking presentation, asking for some help from designer friends at Note-EO. He has rehearsed his main points a thousand times, until he is comfortable with the speech from top to bottom. After attending several of these meetings since he was hired, Aaron also knows that upper-level management will be expecting a particular tone and delivery. With this information, he continues to refine his rehearsal and work on his credibility.

The problem is not Aaron's stage fright but, rather, his limited view on what a presentation can be. Even technical presentations can open the gates for larger change and improvement. With the captive eyes of his management, Aaron has an opportunity to speak personally about what he likes and dislikes at Note-EO. He could offer some suggestions that are close to his heart, and he could show that he is dedicated to the company's long-term growth. It's not very often that he will have a chance to speak his mind so candidly.

Aaron is thinking only about completing the task. He isn't looking ahead. Every presentation is an opportunity to grow, share, and create change.

If Aaron delivers in front of management with his current perspective, he will be an intelligent but otherwise forgettable speaker. They will appreciate that he can clarify all of his main points and has memorized the content of his deck, but they won't know what else is going on in this particular coder's mind.

Navigators like Aaron should look beyond the well-trodden path. How would his presentation differ if he began with a personal story about what it's like to code at Note-EO? What kind of change could he create if they realized the stories behind all of the numbers they see on each slide? An ideal Navigator is able to see different paths, not just one.

YOUR NATURAL HABITAT

Navigators aren't looking for a huge, brightly lit stage. Smaller groups or one-on-one sessions are your strongest natural habitat, where you feel most comfortable engaging in discussion. Because you like to see the results of your labor—that is, positive change—you also prefer environments that encourage you to follow up with your audience, whether through e-mail or in casual conversation at lunch. While small can be great, don't limit yourself! Navigators can make successful TED speakers who inspire full auditoriums and hundreds of thousands of viewers online.

BRAWN (STRENGTHS)

Organized

Focused

Well rounded

You are a straightforward, no-nonsense presenter who is capable of slicing through frilly content and revealing what matters most. When necessary, you can also bring a lot of energy and passion to your talk. This is because you care about the audience as a whole and deeply wish to see positive developments for each individual.

Much of your strength lies in all that extra work you put into preparation. You know you'll be anxious onstage, so you make the effort to rehearse and perfect the flow of your talk. This dedication can cover a lot of flaws, and it helps you come across as credible in front of your audience.

TRAPS (WEAKNESSES)

Timid

Overthinking

Unengaged

Navigators with the best intentions can be brought down by working too closely on one aspect of their presentation without looking at the whole picture. This narrow focus can also affect delivery, where even the most vivacious can become anxious and timid because of their quest for perfection.

Don't forget to add a personal, engaging touch to the overall audience experience. Too much memorization can make you sound stiff or robotic in your delivery. Consider opening your talk with a short, relevant true story. It may help loosen you up and result in a much stronger delivery.

YOUR NATURAL ALLY

Want to gain more insight into Sharing and Durability? Connect with Creators (Chapter 6) to balance your strengths and weaknesses and to see how they approach your weaker quadrants.

YOUR PREY

Because you have a well-rounded presentation style, you appeal to audiences who don't need to see a Broadway show every time they sit down to watch a speech. Your prey are those people who love straightforward, concise information delivered by an everyman presenter, especially when they recognize all the hard work that you put into the design and content of your presentation.

YOUR PREDATORS

You may find it a struggle to inspire or motivate personas that do expect to see something new. Attention spans are short, and even the most receptive audience will have a hard time staying invested if your delivery style is burdened by too much information and few highlights. Even though the concept of "corporate" may be etched deeply in your mind, people are still people. They are driven by their own impatience and desire to be amused.

FIVE DOS AND DON'TS

DOS

1. Consider using an unexpected theme or metaphor within the content of your presentation to show that you went above and beyond the assignment itself.

2. Get creative and become more invested in your presentation by relating and sharing real-life stories that tie into your message.

3. Add some variety by using the entire stage. Stay active, not stationary, while in the spotlight.

4. If you are performing in front of a large group but you feel more comfortable in a small group setting, then learn how to make eye contact with a few key people in the front rows during your talk to simulate that small setting.

5. Practice your speech in a feedback-rich environment, especially with people who are more invested in you than in the presentation. Once you've finished, ask them, "Did I come across as too timid?"

DON'TS

1. Don't rely solely on data to support the main points of your presentation. Include some interesting story-based elements.

2. Don't focus too much on the content or design of a specific slide, but rather focus on the presentation as a whole. Don't obsess over the small details.

3. Don't be held back by fear or insecurity; invite more people to see your presentation. You never know who could benefit from your positive message with a long-term change of mind.

4. Don't put your audience to sleep with an uneventful presentation, Instead, include media enhancements, props, movement, or anything else to liven up your natural straightforward style.

5. Don't just challenge your audience with a call to action. Be sure they are aware of the benefits of listening to your good advice.

THE IDEAL NAVIGATOR

There is no such thing as a bad persona. There are only areas to improve on within your range of strengths and weaknesses. With that in mind, what do ideal Navigators look like?

1. They think outside of the norm to make their presentation more engaging and unexpected while onstage. They might consider using props, videos, or other creative aids to help tell their story in a unique way.

2. They do more than just get the job done. They use a presentation as an opportunity to grow their message and their own abilities.

3. They look beyond their initial speaking assignment, and they find creative ways to make their message stick such as leaving handouts for the audience members and reaching out via social media and e-mail newsletters.

Let's revisit our favorite coder, Aaron, who is anxiously getting ready to deliver a quarterly presentation to his higher-ups. What happens when he refines his ability and becomes an ideal Navigator?

1. He worries less about matching the style of his peers, and he develops his own unique voice.

2. He focuses on his own specific challenges at Note-EO, and he develops a call to action that clearly demonstrates how the company could improve.

3. He uses this presentation as a chance to provide insight into his department, far beyond the data in his slide deck.

There is so much more to presenting than going with the flow. Ideal Navigators travel further than their instinctive path. Instead, they venture into new territory. Like your sea turtle mascot, you are fully prepared for anything that comes your way with a thick shell of rehearsal and preparation to help you. All you need is a fresh view of what your message is capable of achieving with a little imagination and more purpose. Take a risk! Make your message unconventional and loosen those corporate, traditional shackles.

Chapter 13

THE PERFORMER

MEET THE PERFORMER

Imagine adorable circus seals, performing their act with a bright beach ball. They have a radiant energy that draws claps and cheers, wowing the entire audience as they execute tricks in the spotlight. When Performers take to the stage, they achieve a similar effect. They are lit up by an ever-present spotlight generated by their own personality, creating a memorable experience for everyone watching.

If you scored as a Performer, you keep the beach ball spinning with your natural ability to be conversational, funny, and interactive with the audience. While other presenters struggle to be relatable, you have no problem connecting the dots and using storytelling to your advantage. This makes your message naturally more compelling, even when it's about an ordinary topic.

One of the reasons Performers succeed at delivery is that they have a keen set of observational skills. You are able to recognize the signs of a bored, tired, or disengaged audience, and you steer the conversation accordingly. This responsiveness shapes the content of your talk, which means that each time you deliver your message, the content will be slightly different. You might describe this as "keeping things interesting," and it greatly improves the audience experience.

But it's not all claps and cheers for the Performer. When the focus is narrowed to the performance, other aspects of the presentation falter. For example, audience members may struggle to remember crucial facts and main points if they are thinking only about your flashy performance. Performers also tend to ignore the long-term application of their message, either not realizing how to shape their message for memorability or not knowing where to start. Many of these struggles could be eliminated in the Exploration phase, but they are ignored because a Performer's focus is so narrow.

While it is important for presenters to look good onstage and capture the audience's attention, there is still work to be done in delivering an effective and persuasive speech. Successful Performers are able to set aside their personal expectations and ask themselves the serious not-so-fun questions such as, "What are the crucial takeaways of my message?" and "How can I make this session an effective use of my audience's time?" and "How will this message benefit my audience in the long term?"

With just a pinch more practicality and a little less beach ball, Performers have the ability to deliver a presentation that is memorable during and long after the talk itself. You already know how to keep an audience from checking their phones and yawning. All you need is that final push to keep them engaged long after you've walked offstage.

HOW YOU SCORED

The Performer Spotlight (Video):
http://ethos3.com/treats/performer

So how did you score the Performer? These results were calculated using our four-quadrant algorithm in which anything on the outside corner of the specific quadrant is considered high and anything near the main intersection is considered mid-low (Figure 13.1). Here is a simple rundown of your placement in each quadrant and how we arrived at your profile:

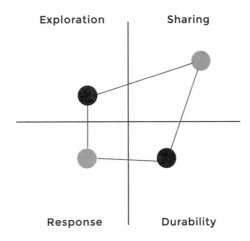

Figure 13.1 The Performer

EXPLORATION

You already know that you are going to do well in front of an audience. This confidence probably stems from years of experience as the class clown or as someone who loves to tell a juicy story around the work lunch table. Because they are confident about their delivery, Performers tend to score in the mid- to low range of Exploration. Performers need to realize that preparation is much more than simple rehearsal. It's about crafting your message, creating materials, and learning how to meet your audience's needs for the long term. We encourage you to work on this area and become familiar with tried-and-true methods of preparation. These include visualization exercises, self-recording, and using a structured script to make sure you stick to your main points and trim any tangents.

SHARING

Performers score extremely well in this quadrant, flexing their best muscle for all to see. Sharing is more than your level of comfort being on-stage. It's also about how energized you become during and after you speak. Anxiety is transformed into energy, and you are able to impress a crowd with a whole range of entertaining tactics. From skilled nonverbal behavior to a mastery of storytelling and humor, this quadrant is by far the strongest and most indicative of your personal style.

RESPONSE

When the speech is finished, Performers feel as if their job is also finished. You scored in the mid- to low range of this quadrant, most likely because you eschew group activities, long discussions, or other more interactive elements of speaking. Why share the spotlight? You probably tend to focus on your own performance rather than the opinions and energy that other people bring to your presentation. While this isn't necessarily a negative thing, it's still important to include everyone in the conversation. Because really, the best presentations feel like a conversation in which different perspectives are expressed, addressed, and valued.

DURABILITY

Because of your narrow focus on Sharing, you scored in the mid- to low range of this quadrant. Perhaps all you need is a fresh view of what a long-term message can look like and how to accomplish that in the future. It's about much more than a single-serve presentation that takes 30 minutes out of the business day. It's about delivering a message that your audience remembers and can use well into the future, influencing future action. How can you get there? How can you make your message more memorable? These are the kinds of questions you will need to answer to improve your score in this quadrant.

SPOTTING A PERFORMER IN THE WILD

Meet Chris, a grad school student in the engineering program at Fromestow University. When people hear the word "engineering," he knows that they want to pull out a comfortable blanket and nap. For his upcoming final project, Chris suspects that the faculty will need to bring tape for their eyelids and a horse's trough of coffee.

But here's the thing about Chris: he comes from a long line of entertainers. He's loud, he's funny, and he's passionate about his chosen career. He would love nothing more than to get a few belly laughs during his final presentation and to give the faculty a break from the monotonous presentations they'll expect from other students.

Chris is so confident that he'll be a crowd pleaser that he isn't even worried about the content of his talk. His prep time is spent sorting through funny stories about his time at Fromestow University, including his different encounters with the faculty. All he needs is a stage and a spotlight, and the audience is guaranteed to remember his talk above those of any of the other students.

The problem is that instead of using his final presentation as a way to show off his skills, make connections, and give himself credibility, Chris is really just using it as a way to show off himself. While he takes the program seriously and does want to succeed, he also needs to refocus his efforts in order to broaden his purpose.

With his vibrant style, he could be using his onstage skills to become a top-of-mind candidate for further career opportunities. Performers like him need to ensure that their performance isn't wasted on the singular goal of entertaining the audience. If Chris wants to entertain the faculty, he will do so naturally. But he also should add a dash of gravity to his presentation and thus use his power for good rather than nothing.

The best place he could start is to provide additional materials that give more information about his final project, which is a bridge design he's been working on during the duration of the program. He could even provide a call to action at the end of his slide deck, providing the professors with ways to further support his long-term vision. And finally, he could fearlessly invite questions from the faculty about the project during his talk, which would prove his credibility and lend weight to his plan.

Sometimes it's about more than just what happens onstage. It's about the seeds that are planted for an offstage harvest.

YOUR NATURAL HABITAT

Center stage is your home, whether the venue is the size of a stadium or a room of five. Your key advantage is the ability to carry over natural

WHAT'S YOUR PRESENTATION PERSONA?

conversational skills from everyday life into a room filled with audience members. The result is that your audience feels more like your friends than people listening politely to an orator.

Use this to your advantage by encouraging more people to attend your talk even if they are in different departments of your company or share different goals. Promise them that they will receive something of value from your talk and deliver on that promise. We don't recommend that you try to share that spotlight with anyone else. Avoid group presentations, if possible.

BRAWN (STRENGTHS)

Personality

Humor

Observational

Your personality adds a lot of value to the messages you deliver, making them more memorable long after the talk is finished. You also have the ability to utilize humor and storytelling depending on the cues your audience gives you. Your strong observational skills help you shape the course of your presentation.

Think of the last time you watched a presenter struggle to remember points or shy away from the audience's gaze. Painful, right? Luckily for Performers, they are equipped to hide any anxious energy, and they appear to be relaxed in front of others.

TRAPS (WEAKNESSES)

Imprecise

Egotistical

Unfocused

You might get the belly laughs you're looking for during a presentation, but without strong actionable takeaways and supportive data, it will lack substance. Without clear guidance and purpose beyond "Watch this," your audience will be distracted from the purpose of your message.

Focusing on your time onstage can cause you to neglect other necessary preparations before a talk. When was the last time you actually sat down and rehearsed a presentation? This extra work may help you become more focused and much more persuasive.

YOUR NATURAL ALLY

Want to learn how to sharpen your preparation skills and make your message last? Meet or observe Curators (Chapter 7), who can help you become a stronger speaker.

YOUR PREY

Anyone suffering from presentation fatigue will be refreshed to see someone with a fun, fresh style of delivery. You appeal to the kind of audience members who have only watched TED talks online and who don't expect something that entertaining to happen at the company's annual budget meeting. Anyone who is distracted easily, dreads presentations, and is stuck in a corporate mindset rut is going to love your style.

YOUR PREDATORS

There's a critic in every audience; most left-brained individuals may be wary of a message that primarily relies on being relatable rather than informative. As in a joke without a punch line, these predators are waiting for you to deliver the facts and stats after you have dazzled them with the storytelling. Make sure that you go into a presentation with a clear purpose, easy-to-digest takeaways, and the proof points you need to convince these hard-boiled critics that there is credibility beneath all of that flash and flair.

FIVE DOS AND DON'TS

DOS

1. Develop a content outline that supports your main idea. If it feels like homework, that's because it is. You will need to provide your audience with something more substantial than great delivery. A logical outline can help you get there.

2. Be sure to support all of your main ideas with one verifiable piece of data, even if it kills you. Your audience will appreciate the dash of credibility.

3. Since you tend to make your materials overly flashy, take a cue from Coco Chanel and remove a few design elements or a couple of extra jokes from your presentation before you leave the house.

4. Keep the humor in your delivery, not on your slides. Funny fonts, images, gifs, and other visual gags can come across as unprofessional, especially when used in large quantities. The best approach is to use humor verbally and then bring the talk back to the main idea or message.

5. Even though you may feel comfortable presenting without rehearsing, you definitely need it in order to polish your message and keep within the right time frame. Aim for at least three full run-throughs of your talk beforehand.

DON'TS

1. Don't forget to address your audience's needs within the content of your message. How can your idea benefit them once the talk is done?

2. You have a tendency to turn a presentation into a routine, so avoid going too far in one direction by limiting your number of stories, jokes, or other irrelevant bits of entertainment.

3. Don't let a tangent take control of your message. If you are sharing a story about yourself to enhance the message, be sure that this section is timed to prevent rambling.

4. Don't let excess energy cause you to rush through a speech. Time yourself, include pauses, and take the opportunity to smell the roses while onstage.

5. Don't forget to include a clear call to action at the end of your speech. Your presentation should have something actionable for your audience to engage with at the end.

THE IDEAL PERFORMER

There is no such thing as a bad persona. There are only areas to improve on within your range of strengths and weaknesses. With that in mind, what do ideal Performers look like?

1. They use their preparation time wisely to unite crucial research with their usual display of storytelling.

2. They consider the long-term impact of their message, and they think of creative ways to shape a call to action that supports that impact. For example, they might ask the audience to do something unexpected, take up a new hobby, or question an existing part of their daily lives to further change.

3. They work hard to give their message substance, providing a clear purpose along with next steps.

Let's revisit the story of Chris, who is a Performer surrounded by Scientists in his engineering program. What happens when he takes a little more time to work on his final project? The results look a little something like this:

1. He designs beautiful takeaway material of his final project, and he gives it out to the entire audience after his talk, along with information about how they can make his vision come true.

2. He includes a Q&A session, and he answers tough questions from his professors, impressing them with his scope of knowledge.

3. He doesn't just deliver an entertaining presentation, one that is more engaging than the presentations his peers deliver. He also is able

to flex his ability as an engineer and make his project the most memorable.

Performers have everything they need to keep an audience transfixed on their spinning red beach ball. Where other personas struggle to impress onstage, they are effortless and fun to watch. The only potential problems lie with the substance of their talk and their purpose as a whole. What are you trying to accomplish? What do you want the audience to walk away remembering? Once you've answered these questions for yourself, make sure that the audience also knows your purpose. Even if you have to splash them with water and repeat it five times, you're the right seal for the job.

Chapter 14

THE PRODUCER

MEET THE PRODUCER

Imagine a rhino roaming the savannah: a creature that demands respect but also gives off a distinct "look but don't touch" vibe. It's an impressive sight, but it's not one you want to get especially close to and snap a few selfies with. Similarly, Producers demand the respect of their audience, but they exude a sense of authority that doesn't encourage conversation or questions. They are strong presenters who command the stage with the weight of their presence. And perhaps the size of their horns?

One of the reasons Producers are so credible and impressive is that they carefully prepare beforehand. It's hard to argue with a presentation filled with supporting facts, sourced stats, and proof points around every corner. They also spend time getting to the audience's needs, ensuring that potential questions are addressed during their talk.

That point is important to remember, that questions are often addressed *during* their talk. Producers don't spend a lot of time, or perhaps any time, on group activities, Q&A sessions, and other elements of a presentation that rely on audience participation. This might be because they are used to the traditional idea of a presentation, in which presenters take the stage, deliver their speech, and then step down when they're finished.

But it could also be due to a discomfort with discussion or an unwillingness to hear outside opinions and potential questions.

If you scored as the Producer persona, you may have a range of reasons why you've never chosen to encourage discussion after your talk. You may also be surprised to hear that avoiding audience interaction can make you seem a little distant. Sometimes this can work to your advantage, especially if you want to appear like the final authority on the content of your talk. But sometimes, it might be good to hear some outside opinions on your message—even if you're hearing from a presentation persona assessment.

Another trait that Producers share that makes them so memorable is their ability to shape their message into something that has long-term value. Say, for instance, they have an investor pitch for a product they are developing. Producers are creative enough to think beyond a few initial presentations, and they consider ways that the slide deck can be used well into the future, in front of other audiences. In general, they tend to think big.

Producers are fantastic presenters and "beasts" onstage. But you can always become stronger and work toward making personal connections with your specific audience. Let them know that your horns are merely decorative, and give them an opportunity to speak or interact with you when possible. With just a pinch of improvement, you can become the strongest speaker in the savannah.

HOW YOU SCORED

The Producer Spotlight (Video):
http://ethos3.com/treats/producer

So how did you score the Producer? These results were calculated using our four-quadrant algorithm in which anything on the outside corner of the specific quadrant is considered high and anything near the main intersection is considered mid-low (Figure 14.1). Here is a simple rundown of your placement in each quadrant and how we arrived at your profile:

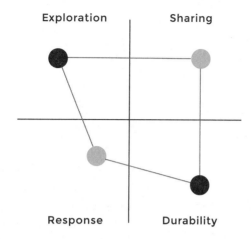

Figure 14.1 The Producer

EXPLORATION

Producers score well in this quadrant, landing in the mid- to high range of the plot. If there is a task to be done, you are willing to roll up your sleeves and get to work. Similarly, you aren't afraid to devote as much time as necessary to ensure that your presentation is a success. Whether it's collecting powerful quotes, finding important supportive data, or Googling exactly who will be in your audience, Producers put in the extra effort before they step onstage so that they will appear knowledgeable to their audience and feel confident in themselves.

SHARING

With all of their wisdom, preparedness, and authority, it's not surprising that Producers score in the mid- to high range of this quadrant. You know the points that you want to make, and then you deliver them with conviction. Your audience is never unclear about what the main purpose of your talk is or what they are expected and/or encouraged to do once the talk is finished. Other personas might score high in Sharing because of their conversational and fun tone, but you really score well here because you don't waste the audience's time. You say what you mean to say, back it up with proof, and then leave the audience feeling well educated on the topic.

RESPONSE

This is the only area that Producers struggle in, averaging scores in the mid- to low range of the quadrant. Why? A lot of this area has to do with the information that the audience has immediately after the talk is finished and whether you spend time interacting with them. Since there are so many different learning styles and perspectives that may not adhere to yours, it's important to customize your message in this crucial stage. Mingling with your audience, ensuring that they are engaged, and using relevant group activities are all ways to improve their internal response during and after the presentation.

DURABILITY

Producers like their messages to mean something. They want to create long-term change or significantly alter the way their audience thinks. For most, a speaking opportunity is wasted unless it causes significant and positive change in the world. This instinct is why Producers score in the high range of the Durability quadrant: they are big-idea thinkers with the desire and energy to make their presentation an opportunity for so much *more*.

SPOTTING A PRODUCER IN THE WILD

Meet Jeff, the CEO of a midsize financial company called X-9 Invest. He's no backseat CEO but, rather, a hands-on leader who loves his business and works hard to understand his employees' needs. Every year, he delivers a keynote address to the company to keep everyone informed about new policies, company performance, and other miscellaneous changes that each department needs to know about.

Jeff works hard on this presentation. He locks himself up in his office for a week and writes his speech, designs his slides, and rehearses in front of a mirror. He runs through stories about X-9 Invest employees who have done impressive work during the year, and he even peppers the talk with a few jokes. His goal is to deliver something fast, to the point, yet still fun. He knows that his team will be looking forward to the free catered lunch, and he doesn't want to waste their time or seem like the kind of CEO who loves to hear himself talk.

Every year, his presentation goes smoothly. He starts and ends in the allotted time, says what he needs to say, and comes across as a credible and thoughtful leader. His team enjoys it, and they remember his main points throughout the year because of the initiatives he establishes.

But there is room for Jeff to improve. At present, these talks are a bit like a doctor's: clean, sterile, and effective but not somewhere that you would really want to spend a lot of time. Jeff is missing a great opportunity to connect with his team and hear voices from different departments. He might give each of the departments a portion of time to speak, or he could open up the floor to questions. He could also create some group activities or introduce a think tank to present ideas they've already been prepped on before the talk.

These annual talks require that every employee attend. This is a huge opportunity to bring the team together in a social way, even if it deviates a little from Jeff's rigid schedule. Adding in a more conversational feel can also help new employees see Jeff in a different light, as someone approachable.

In a single presentation, a CEO has the chance to break down barriers between what people assume a CEO is like and the kind of guy Jeff actually is at his core. He needs to look beyond time efficiency to consider ways to encourage meaningful interactions between himself and his team.

He is already putting in the necessary work to deliver a presentation that gets the job done. All Jeff needs is a little nudge in the right direction to make his talk more engaging, more interactive, and thus more meaningful. As a Producer, his goal should always be to "produce" a stronger connection between himself and his audience.

YOUR NATURAL HABITAT

What does a rhino have to fear? Group size doesn't tend to worry you unless you're concerned your message won't be heard by the right people.

Most Producers are comfortable in a setting large enough that they can end their talk and walk out the door afterward. *Elvis has left the building.* If this sounds familiar, consider moving outside of your comfort zone and scheduling a brief 10-minute discussion after your talk to leave the audience with a more personal ending.

BRAWN (STRENGTHS)

Clever

Impactful

Knowledgeable

Your messages have long-term impact, and they are ready to stand on a global stage. Why? Producers are excellent at preparing these messages beforehand, and they also have an effective presence onstage. This is due to a crucial combination of the following: natural ability, a perspective that makes you take your assignment seriously, ambition, and the intelligence to take your message to the next level.

The "clever" strength also comes from an inherent knowledge of audience needs. As we mentioned in "Meet the Producer," you pepper your presentation with exactly what your listeners expect and want to hear throughout your talk. Is this due to past experience as a speaker? Perhaps it's because of your own expectations of yourself. Either way, you're a smart speaker who knows how to accomplish your onstage goals.

TRAPS (WEAKNESSES)

Impersonal

Unhelpful

Intimidating

There is a span of time immediately after the presentation that offers the speaker a chance to address concerns, reaffirm the call to action, and network to make important connections. Producers tend to roll their eyes at this crucial step and are instead focused on the next big thing. This can give audiences a chill and also hurt their short-term understanding of the message.

Perhaps even more than this, not spending time to work on the Response quadrant can leave people feeling left out. If you do an excellent job and then flee, your audience may suspect that the presentation was an item on the to-do list. Make sure you reiterate that your audience is valuable and that you are interested in hearing what they have to say.

YOUR NATURAL ALLY

Take a lesson from Befrienders (Chapter 4) either by connecting in person or by observing one in action. They can help you improve your Response.

YOUR PREY

Some people like to chew their food slowly, savoring the flavor and appreciating the quality of the cooking. Those same careful, thoughtful people are the kinds of audience members who will love you. They will understand your message at first glance, and they will follow through in the long term by remembering what you said. You won't have to worry about interacting with these slow chewers; they can fill the gap of knowledge using just the information provided during the speech.

YOUR PREDATORS

In contrast to the more self-guided members of your audience, there will always be those who need extra clarification and a little bit of hand-holding. Cater to them by eliminating jargon, simplifying your main points and takeaways, and creating some interactive moments even if it kills you. Don't just aim to come across as powerful and experienced; seek to become more approachable and friendly in your next big presentation.

FIVE DOS AND DON'TS

DOS

1. You know that your message has long-term value, but you need to also make sure that you convey its benefits for the short term. Your audience will be more likely to act if they can imagine results tomorrow, next week, or even next month.

2. Add more meaning to your message by editing its underlying purpose. How can your takeaways, research, and hard work all add up to a change in your audience? Keep the word "change" in mind as you revise.

3. Prevent a zoned-out audience by throwing in a few surprise elements: props, a pinch of humor, or a story.

4. Group activities don't have to be a drag. Consider events you've gone to that have had fun group activities. Take inspiration from those no matter how unusual or out of the box they seem to be.

5. Do you schedule time at the end of your presentation to address audience questions? If you don't, start today. If you already do, stretch out that time to incorporate more audience interactivity. It's a great way to get your audience personally involved with the message.

DON'TS

1. Don't doubt your ability to persuade an audience. You have everything it takes! You put in the research, you have a long-term message, and you have some solid delivery skills. All of this adds up to the ability to turn a "no" into a "yes."

2. Don't hide your main points in a cloud of jargon and technical terminology. The most effective speakers, such as Steve Jobs, use fifth-grade vocabulary to make their points more relatable and clear.

3. Don't forget to smile! Producers are often serious, no-nonsense presenters. If you find it hard to come across as personable, include a short story that makes you smile to retell it and open your talk with it.

4. Don't neglect to use your presentation as a networking opportunity. Invite people you've never met in person and tell them to bring their friends.

5. Don't feel like you've failed if an audience member asks for clarification on a main point during or after your talk. Use it as an opportunity in the future to edit your content and home in on the right message.

THE IDEAL PRODUCER

There is no such thing as a bad persona. There are only areas to improve on within your range of strengths and weaknesses. With that in mind, what do ideal Producers look like?

1. They put their audience first, well above their message, in order to break down barriers between them and their audience.

2. They schedule time after or even during their presentation to accommodate a group activity, discussion, or specific Q&A session.

3. They ignore the clock and instead aim to finish their presentation when everyone in the room is engaged and satisfied with the message itself.

Let's revisit Jeff, our thorough CEO who plans to deliver his annual keynote speech. What happens when he takes inspiration from a few of our lessons and applies it to his presentation?

1. He lets his audience know beforehand that they are encouraged to bring opinions about past initiatives and that he will host an optional Q&A to help the team better understand his thinking and decision-making in the past and future.

2. He shares the spotlight with team members so that they can tell their own stories rather than try to describe them himself.

3. He shortens his speech to make time for small group discussions across each department, focused on what they loved and hated over the past year.

Powerful presenters can sometimes be intimidating—like rhinos. Whenever possible, Producers should be aware of ways to humanize their message and allow the audience to speak for themselves. They need to make it clear that the audience is important and that it is not merely about their own clout and purpose. There are so many ways that this can be accomplished and the spotlight can be shared. Also, Producers already have the creativity to ensure that it can work for their own message. Show your audience how empathetic and invested you can be.

Chapter 15

THE SCHOLAR

MEET THE SCHOLAR

A Scholar steps onto a stage in front of a large audience. The room is quiet, waiting for her to begin. She walks to the lectern and sets down a thick pile of notes that corresponds with each slide of her presentation. Although she is not a natural performer, she has the information she needs to feel confident. Or perhaps, considering the sweat on her collar, she is just "confident-ish."

Her presentation is data-driven and to the point. The audience listens respectfully, impressed by how much the Scholar has prepared for the event. Of course, a few audience members check their iPhones to see what's on the menu at Panera for lunch. But in general, the presentation is delivered smoothly and without any major problems. Well researched and fully prepared—that's the Scholarly way.

The Scholar is represented by the owl, which has always been a symbol for the wise, curious, and studious among us.

If you received the Scholar profile, it indicates that you tend to put in the extra research and time to make your presentations powerful. Your content also benefits from the knowledge you have gathered over the years. You are an intellectual speaker who knows what you are talking about. Messages you deliver also have staying power, especially when they are paired with statements, numbers, or facts that inspire awe.

Scholars have the ability to make an unexpectedly strong pitch as long as they are able to organize their excess and direct the presentation to a singular call to action or final point. The word *edit* should be your nearest and dearest friend as you revise notes or content on your slides. The more you cut, the more you'll be able to cut to the chase during your talk.

However, Scholars are not without their weaknesses. All of the facts and stats in the world can't spare you from delivering a dull performance or being unpersuasive if you aren't cautious. Avoid data dumps at all costs. They may leave your audience impressed with your Excel chart abilities and little else. You also should be wary of coming across as uninvested or even uninterested in your message, both of which you can avoid with the use of storytelling, emotion, or just a pinch of delivery flair.

When done correctly, being a Scholar positions you as a uniquely authoritative figure. The following is geared to help you overcome common challenges for your persona. You should note that every Scholar will be slightly different, and some of these messages may hit home while others may not. The goal is simply to break you out of your well-researched, studious little shell. The result? A whip smart presenter with the ability to drop numbers, when appropriate, to support his or her message. We believe in you.

HOW YOU SCORED

The Scholar Spotlight (Video):
http://ethos3.com/treats/scholar

So how did you score the Scholar? These results were calculated using our four-quadrant algorithm in which anything on the outside corner of the specific quadrant is considered high and anything near the main intersection is considered mid-low (Figure 15.1). Here is a simple rundown of your placement in each quadrant and how we arrived at your profile:

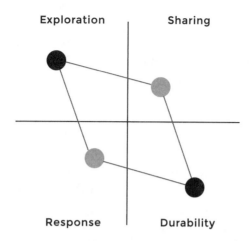

Figure 15.1 The Scholar

EXPLORATION

You scored high in this area, as most Scholars tend to put a hefty amount of work into their exploration of a subject. They crunch numbers, cite sources, and make sure that they are well rehearsed beforehand. They also have a tendency to create multiple drafts of their presentation storyboard, although design does not take center stage in their preparation.

SHARING

Most Scholars tend to be humble about this experience or downright nervous the entire time. You scored much lower in this quadrant than you did in Exploration, which could be due to a number of factors. Nervousness, inexperience, and natural comfort onstage all play a role in this category. Scholars need a lot of work in this area, and most likely already know it.

RESPONSE

Scholars tend to do a good to sometimes just-OK job in this area. They may mingle with the crowd and answer a few spontaneous questions, but they don't often have an extensive plan for follow-up after the talk. Most are just happy it's over. However, it's important to improve in this area: networking can strengthen a message, and Q&A sessions will please extroverts, who make up most of your crowd.

DURABILITY

Because you put so much work into your research, your messages tend to have longevity and relevance for the future. People will remember and pay attention to what you said long after the presentation was delivered. A long-term reward is often the fruit of early labor in the preparation stage. Both these strengths create aha moments for your audience that lasts long after the talk is over.

SPOTTING A SCHOLAR IN THE WILD

Meet Jenny, a number cruncher at a huge corporation that produces expensive headphones. She was given the task to deliver an annual "how are we doing" presentation with her findings for the year. Because she's worked at the company for five years now, she plans to use her go-to approach of charts, graphs, and stats.

But here's the thing: this year, she knows that the numbers indicate that a certain line of headphones should be cut from production. Jenny feels that all of the proof is there and that the numbers on her slides will point the audience in the right direction. To back up her point, she ensures that each slide is crammed with information about that particular headphone line.

Jenny has the right intentions and is correct in thinking that her higher-ups will want proof about this new information. But her approach is wrong. Data isn't going to jump off the slide and slap her audience in the face. It's her job to do that with a presentation delivery or design that works in tandem with her message.

This is a classic Scholar move: to put everything on a slide, stand back, and say, "Look at this," expecting the audience to be convinced. While some members of the audience may take the time to read through a slide and catch her meaning, most will need a little more explanation to understand the information fully.

The best way she could improve her presentation would be to be clear about her primary point, that a line of headphones should be cut. That fact alone could (and should!) take up its own slide to be placed at the beginning and end of the presentation and perhaps even mentioned again in the middle. It doesn't mean she has to eliminate stats, but the stats should always act in a supporting role to the main purpose.

Jenny needs to make it short and sweet. She has all of the information she needs to convince her audience, which for many other personalities is the most difficult first step.

A Scholar with a clear goal and the right data can be unstoppable. If Jenny heeds our advice in this situation, she will probably surprise higher-ups with a change in pacing, and she will probably get them to pay attention. She will also accomplish her most important goal, which is to call attention to a specific data anomaly that will lead to companywide change. And she will retain her thorough, well-backed style. That's how an ideal Scholar works.

YOUR NATURAL HABITAT

Scholars prefer to speak in front of people who are already interested and willing to learn something new, such as in a classroom type of environment. The size of the audience doesn't matter because interaction is a low priority.

While you may be anxious about public speaking, it will be counterbalanced by the fact that you want a large number of people to be exposed to new concepts and innovative ideas. You would feel satisfied if the audience was able to share the way you felt about the topic or if they walked away with a working knowledge of the main points. We call this "closing the knowledge gap," which describes the space between "I don't know anything about this topic" and "I feel interested and motivated about this topic." In short, your ideal natural habitat would be on the TED stage or a similar large-scale educational venue.

BRAWN (STRENGTHS)

Detail oriented

Factual

Curious

Many other presenters tend to halfheartedly do their research, gather facts, or make sure their claims are credible, but not you. You are more than willing to put in the extra work to make your speech accurate and thorough, no matter the topic. For you, detail-oriented work and passion go hand-in-hand. This puts you at a large advantage with content that stands on its own without any "flashiness" required to cover flaws in logic or flow.

Well-backed points also hold up the most strongly against critique, and you will be ready to face any question that a Q&A can throw at you. Use this to your advantage and keep an arsenal of information nearby that doesn't appear in your presentation but can live in speaker's notes. The audience doesn't always need to see your winning hand, and luckily for Scholars, an ace is always handy in the form of great research.

TRAPS (WEAKNESSES)

Unemotional

Not persuasive

Boring

The facts and stats will naturally be there to support your message, but Scholars can struggle with bringing emotion to the stage. A lack of stories, using little persuasiveness, or simply not being relatable can hurt a presenter who sometimes values being correct more than sharing something meaningful.

The problem is not your intent or even your own ability. Most often, Scholars are simply including too much information in their presentations.

Audiences can only remember so much. If you really feel drawn to giving them a car owner's manual of data, consider using a takeaway document that you can hand out afterward. Otherwise, let your data home in on specific points that support your argument without weighing down your talk.

YOUR NATURAL ALLY

Want to learn how to spice up your Sharing and increase your Response? Take lessons from Activators (Chapter 2) and improve your skills while helping them strengthen theirs.

YOUR PREY

Students, armchair learners, and people who are generally curious will be enthusiastic about your message and eager to examine the data for themselves later. You can lure these learners to your presentation by creating promotional materials that boldly advertise, "Lessons will be taught here!" Even though we advocate simplicity and respecting your audience's memory space, there will always be those in the audience who love to be dazzled by facts and figures. You have a natural foothold with these lifelong learners: use that to your advantage to attract as many as you can to your next speech.

YOUR PREDATORS

Audience members who are Performers or Activators expect to be energized by other storytellers like themselves when they walk into the room, and they are at risk of falling asleep during your talk. It's just a fact that not everyone will enjoy your facts. Work toward creating an emotional connection with your audience alongside the compelling, stat-heavy, chart-filled presentation to appeal to a broad range of personalities.

FIVE DOS AND DON'TS

DOS

1. Be mindful of the fact that presentations exist to persuade. Even if you want to educate your audience about a topic, you also should be persuading them to take on a new perspective or gain a new frame of mind.

2. Inject some emotion into your talk by sharing a relevant story about yourself. Consider answering these unspoken questions to prepare: Why are you onstage today? What makes this message dear to your heart? How did you come up with this idea?

3. Make your presentation more engaging by including an interesting handout, prop, or some uniquely designed slides to wow the audience during your speech.

4. Smile, move around the entire stage, make eye contact with your audience, and use hand gestures to keep from coming across as robotic. Remember, it's not just a lecture. You are selling yourself on that stage.

5. You work hard on organizing your presentation and supporting your main points with credible data. Try spending an equal amount of energy on rehearsing your delivery to engage your audience.

DON'TS

1. Don't be a reactive presenter. Think outside the box. Try to deliver a kind of presentation that *you've* never seen before.

2. Don't drown your talk with data, facts, and stats. Each main point needs a supporting point but often no more than that. Audiences tend not to remember more than three points, so cater to their poor memory and spend more time talking about high-level concepts than nitty-gritty percentages and charts.

3. Don't neglect to use high-quality photographs and other visual aids on your slides. Charts and bullet points alone will put your audience to sleep.

4. Don't include more than three important takeaways for your audience to remember after the talk. Trust us, they won't remember any more than three.

5. Even if your presentation is meant primarily to be educational, don't leave out a call to action at the end. Give your audience such an exciting rallying cry that they jump out of their chairs to accomplish it when the talk is finished.

THE IDEAL SCHOLAR

There is no such thing as a bad persona. There are only areas to improve on within your range of strengths and weaknesses. With that in mind, what do ideal Scholars look like?

1. They are capable of using the right data at the right time. They know how to present the information beautifully in a way that captivates and supports their main points rather than overwhelming their audience.

2. They move past their belief that research alone is enough to prepare for a presentation, and they are able to enhance their delivery with more personal touches to become more engaging presenters.

3. They gives their audience a compelling call to action by building up all of their information to support a final argument.

Let's look back at Jenny, the data-loving employee who is going to present in front of her higher-ups. When she follows these tips, here's how her revised presentation goes:

1. She works to make her message more engaging by relying on talking points that support the information rather than a lot of text on the slides.

2. She starts with the most crucial point, showing the necessary information in bold text on one of the first slides. This makes it clear to her audience that while a summary of the fiscal year is important, it has also revealed something more important that needs to be changed.

3. She creates a final slide that conveys her suggestion to the higher-ups in light of the information presented. In this case, the words on the slide will simply say, "We need to cut production of Headphone X."

The result? Her bosses are convinced, impressed, and ready to take the necessary steps to follow her advice. Scholars can easily sell their audience on an idea or change minds as long as they are willing to make the data work for them, not against them.

Changing your perspective is how you are going to evolve from being a mere barn owl to becoming a fearsome bird of prey. Now, get out there and be the best Scholar you can be.

Chapter 16

THE SCIENTIST

MEET THE SCIENTIST

C onsider all of the best qualities of a mouse: intelligent, driven, and capable of solving any maze for the sake of that delicious piece of cheese at the end. The mouse is not worried about the work that might be involved along the way, whether it's another puzzle to solve or a wheel to run on. In a similar way, Scientists are willing to put in as much work as necessary to accomplish their goal. The end result? If not cheese, definitely a well-informed and impressed audience.

Preparation is a Scientist's specialty. A formula for preparation might look a little something like this: research, storyboard, design, rehearse, and repeat. Scientists don't worry about how long this process might take; instead remain focused on doing a thorough job to prepare themselves before they step onstage. They calculate audience needs, they are fully aware of what is expected from them, and they devote themselves to fine-tuning their message and design.

If you scored as a Scientist, you might be a master of thorough preparation in other areas of your life. Maybe you're the kind of person who likes to read the instruction manual before playing a board game. Perhaps you like watching how-to videos online. In any case, "attention to detail" are three words that don't scare you. This is one of your best qualities, especially because we believe that the bulk of a great presentation is set up before a speaker even steps onstage.

What happens when a Scientist presents? The results can be mixed because they are often weighed down by the bulk of their own efforts. With so much research, so many data points, and so much detail, Scientists can fumble as they worry about missing important information.

A narrow focus on the data rather than on the impact of a speech can also hurt an audience's memory of the main points. Sometimes too much is just too much. No one hearing Scientists doubts that they know their stuff. The problem lies in transmitting this knowledge in a clear way to the audience.

If you struggle with getting the audience to leave satisfied and fully informed, your focus needs to shift away from preparation and toward the audience. How can you simplify your message without talking down to them? How can you edit your data, facts, and stats to include only the most relevant information? Sometimes it's about putting down that clipboard, setting aside that beaker, and focusing on what the audience experiences rather than showcasing how much research you put into the talk.

HOW YOU SCORED

The Scientist Spotlight (Video):
http://ethos3.com/treats/scientist

So how did you score the Scientist? These results were calculated using our four-quadrant algorithm in which anything on the outside corner of the specific quadrant is considered high and anything near the main intersection is considered mid-low (Figure 16.1). Here is a simple rundown of your placement in each quadrant and how we arrived at your profile:

EXPLORATION

Scientists score in the highest possible area of this quadrant, with a value so high that it almost breaks through the chart itself. More than just preparedness, Scientists also have a broad comprehension of what the expectations

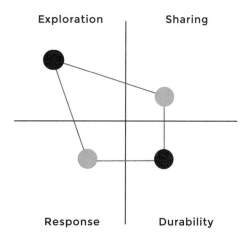

Figure 16.1 The Scientist

for their speech might be. They know how high the stakes are, and they also know exactly what the repercussions of either success or failure can be. This knowledge greatly affects the time they put into researching their topic, creating a content storyboard, designing the slide deck, and rehearsing the presentation out loud. As a Scientist, you can see all of the different chess pieces and potential moves on the table. You use Exploration as a way to make the right choices for every move you accomplish.

SHARING

When the stakes are high, the stress is high. Scientists fall in the mid- to low range of this quadrant, perhaps because of an overload of information and the high pressure that they put on themselves. It's hard to seem natural when you are struggling to remember paragraphs of a speech or strings of information. You don't lack ability or drive to do well in Sharing, which should be much more about having a conversation with your audience than becoming an auctioneer of facts and stats. When Scientists are able to let go of this, they perform much better.

RESPONSE

You might think of this quadrant as the second half of Sharing, so Scientists fall into the mid- to low range of this category as well. Are you uncomfortable hosting a Q&A? Unsure how to answer difficult questions or wrap up a presentation? Preparing for a strong immediate response is all about ad-libbing with your audience, which memorization can't help you with. Instead of rehearsing alone in front of the mirror, buy a friend a drink and talk over your main points. Answer his or her questions and become comfortable discussing your topic in a more natural way. Then, when the big day arrives, you'll already have experience chatting about your subject rather than just delivering it.

DURABILITY

This quadrant might pose some revolutionary ideas to Scientists, who tend to score in the mid- to low range. What if your audience took the information that they learned and applied it in a real-life way? What if they were able to remember your message long after the talk was finished? In order to make a message durable, Scientists need to edit the content of their message from the Exploration stage. They need to learn ways to twist, shape, and mold their message into something much broader and longer-lasting. Not sure how this might work? Check out Chapter 22 about Quadrant 4 later on in the book.

SPOTTING A SCIENTIST IN THE WILD

Meet Lilly, a reporter at a local publication called *The Daily Tuba*. She's new to a small team of seasoned reporters. She is also new to the city, which makes her feel intimidated in her starting position.

What sets Lilly apart, however, is her drive. She's a thorough writer who makes sure that every single one of her facts and sources is vetted before putting a word down on paper. She is also a fast learner, and she is highly motivated to become one of the best reporters at *The Daily Tuba*.

Every month, the team meets for a session during which the reporters pitch ideas to the editorial staff for long-running pieces or monthly features. The best one or two ideas are adopted, and special real estate is made available for these features online and in the printed paper.

Lilly has an idea to run a feature about adjunct professors in her town. She is convinced that there is something fishy going on with the percentage of tenured professors and the number of recent adjunct additions that come and go through a revolving door. While the story is interesting, the problem is that she wants almost double the normal feature space to accommodate all of the testimonies and other information she's already uncovered.

To convince the editors that the extra space will be worth it, she's prepared a presentation to show some of the most shocking stats her research has revealed. She has a set of quotes, images, copies of pay stubs, and student interview footage that she wants to include in her deck to support her case. The problem is that Lilly has compiled too much information, and her editors will suspect that her article will need to be edited in the same way that her presentation needs some pruning.

Lilly needs to put on an editing lens rather than her normal research-driven reporter lens. She needs to look objectively at the content that she has acquired to find the emotionally compelling information. Overwhelming her audience is not going to convince them that she deserves more room in the newspaper. She needs to make her point clear, draw the editors in with compelling information, and then end the presentation with her main point repeated for emphasis.

Lilly is an underdog, but she's also a Scientist. She already has everything she needs to make a convincing case. For most people, gathering information is the hard part. For Lilly, her challenge will be to edit everything down to what is essential to persuade her editors to give this story a huge feature. Perhaps the only thing that stands between a Scientist and success is a shift in perspective from asking, "How do I prove my point?" to "How can I make my audience *feel* the same way I do?"

YOUR NATURAL HABITAT

Small crowds, large crowds, and medium-size crowds, oh my! Scientists are usually anxious about any number of people watching their presentation, but they feel a little more comfortable when the group is large enough that they don't have to answer questions or mingle afterward. Embrace this fear by leaving your audience with materials that don't require a guide, such as handouts with more information or other valuable takeaway resources. That way your audience will feel satisfied and not abandoned with the information you presented.

BRAWN (STRENGTHS)

Thorough

Dedicated

Prepared

Your search history is miles long before you even type a word into a PowerPoint document, and you know how to cite your sources. Scientists are one of the most thorough and invested personalities when it comes to creating a content storyboard or designing their presentations; no topic is too difficult, no amount of research too small. It's this can-do attitude that separates you from the crowd and gives you an unbeatable dedication to your message.

"Dedication" is the key word here. While other people may go through the motions of preparation in order to get the project over with, you work hard because, frankly, you enjoy it. You like being able to tinker with content and design until it feels just right, and you appreciate the joy of a well-sourced document that is watertight.

TRAPS (WEAKNESSES)

Anxious

Momentary

Uptight

What happens when the best formula fails? Sometimes the act of preparation does not create the desired results; there are just too many unknown factors. Scientists' presentations risk coming across as too data heavy to be memorable, and Scientists seem to be too focused on their materials to be relatable. Don't just work on the tangible facts but rather work to prepare for the theoretical events that could happen during your talk. Random questions, a quiet room, and unengaged audience members are included in this list. In short, prepare for anything that can't be easily Googled.

Scientists also struggle with being natural and conversational onstage. It's not easy to be yourself when a group of people, perhaps even a group of scary strangers, are staring at you. However, tactics such as starting with a personal story and peppering your talk with personal details may help ease you through the speech, and they may also help you appear more relaxed.

YOUR NATURAL ALLY

Take a lesson from Captivators (Chapter 5) and find inspiration in their ability to perform well onstage. Watch, listen, and interact with any Captivators you can find.

YOUR PREY

You appeal primarily to other research devotees, such as Curators, Scholars, and Navigators, who will recognize and appreciate your thorough work. These are the personalities who love to see sources cited and can recognize when you've spent time rehearsing main points over and over. Give them a reason to launch into a standing ovation at the end of your talk by making a call to action that appeals to the lifelong learners in your midst.

YOUR PREDATORS

Sweet and salty, good cop and bad cop. People love to have a balance of serious and "fluffy" when it comes to a presentation, as with any performance or educational experience. Audience members who search for levity within your presentation and find none may be disappointed, but they are also less likely to remember your main points.

FIVE DOS AND DON'TS

DOS

1. Add a friendly, warm element to your talk by sharing a story that shows your audience why the subject matter excites you.

2. Chances are, you're putting way too many takeaways into your presentation for anyone to remember. Good Scientists know when they are at risk of overwhelming their audience, and they can edit their points accordingly.

3. After you finish the first draft of your presentation, write down a list of potential audience questions about the content itself. Can you answer these during your talk? If it's a "maybe," consider adding a Q&A session to facilitate better audience comprehension.

4. Always make eye contact. Break the room into three sections and take time to focus on one person in each section. Rinse and repeat.

5. When was the last time you devoted preparation time to rehearsing the delivery? More than that, when was the last time you actively asked for feedback on your delivery? Be sure to spend a little more time polishing your onstage performance.

DON'TS

1. Don't ignore your audience's needs. What are they getting out of your talk? How can you ensure that they walk away thinking, "I gained a new perspective, and I love it."

2. Don't forget that a presentation can be more than just informative. It can be used as a powerful tool for persuasion. How can your message change hearts and minds? How can it improve the lives of those who watch it?

3. Don't let your slides be the star of your presentation. They may be informative and beautiful, but they will rely on the strength of a great presenter to make them memorable.

4. Don't include so much content and so many slides that you need to rush to meet your time limit. Timed rehearsals and careful editing can help prevent a speedy style.

5. Don't let research eat up the bulk of your preparation efforts. Divide your time equally between delivery rehearsal, audience research, and presentation content and design.

THE IDEAL SCIENTIST

There is no such thing as a bad persona. There are only areas to improve on within your range of strengths and weaknesses. With that in mind, what do ideal Scientists look like?

1. They are able to edit the unnecessary within their presentation, trimming it down to be as clear and simple as possible.

2. They refocus their goal away from displaying their hard work to evoking emotion in their audience.

3. They adopt a more conversational tone to make their delivery more natural, including tactics such as storytelling and using nonverbal cues to exude warmth.

Let's revisit Lilly, our motivated reporter from *The Daily Tuba*. What happens when she changes her perspective and works on becoming the ideal Scientist?

1. She cuts her presentation in half and limits her sources to a single compelling story, which gives her deck a strategic focus on what matters.

2. She starts the presentation with a personal story about her experience talking to an adjunct professor with a large family who is trying to make ends meet.

3. She invites questions after her presentation to address concerns about the length of her article, which gives her credibility and impresses the team.

When ideal Scientists step back from their own mountain of work and view that same mountain through the audience's eyes, they are able to make the changes they need to improve as presenters. Sometimes it's less about asking *how* and more about asking *why*. Scientists have an advantage that many presenters don't in that they are capable and willing to understand both. It's important that you not let the "how" take over, devouring the content of your talk and distracting you and your audience from what really matters.

Chapter 17

THE SOLDIER

MEET THE SOLDIER

S oldiers never falter with their message. Like ants driven to feed their queen, they are inspired by a single purpose and are reluctant to venture off the narrow path. In the presentation realm, this translates into a persona who loves important causes to champion. Soldiers are megaphones for everything that they love, from a brand to a lifestyle philosophy. In everything they do, focusing on the big picture is always top of mind. What's good for the single ant is probably good for the entire colony, and they are excited to spread the word.

The characteristic of Soldiers is the ability to create a road map for themselves and others to show how their call to action can be achieved. They have a lofty end goal with a dream of a large platform, but they are also practical enough to know how to get there. You can recognize Soldiers by their emphasis on the future, always painting a vision for themselves and others to enjoy. If it's original, focused on widespread change, and delivered by someone who is optimistic about the future, it's a presentation by a Soldier.

If you scored this persona, you are probably someone who questions excessive presentation design, group activities, and other creative additions to a message that may detract from the larger vision. Maybe you like to keep your message simple, or perhaps you aren't sure what add-ons could actually provide value to your cause. If the most important goal is extending your platform, why bother with the fluff and frills?

This minimal approach to presentation content, design, and delivery is great for your audience's long-term memory of your speech. But what about the time before, during, and immediately after your talk? Soldiers' focus on the end goal can harm them in surprising ways. They struggle to deliver engaging, lively presentations. It's the difference between teaching a person $2 \times 2 = 4$ and using a catchy song to help teach multiplication. Soldiers provide facts and facts alone.

Adding just a pinch of fun will help the audience enjoy your talk. Even the most serious corporate audience is still made up of people with short attention spans, drifting minds, hopes and dreams, and a secret wish for lunch to come quickly. A great message is critical, but it's equally important to address your audience as flesh-and-blood human beings. How will your long-term vision affect their lives? How can you share some of your own excitement that led you to choose this particular message?

With a slight refocusing from the long-term view to the shorter-term view that includes the more immediate needs of the audience, Soldiers can become unstoppable. Frills can be fun! With your newly revised stance and flashy presentation, you may find that you enjoy your mission more than you thought possible. Carry on, Soldier!

HOW YOU SCORED

The Solider Spotlight (Video):
http://ethos3.com/treats/soldier

So how did you score the Soldier? These results were calculated using our four-quadrant algorithm in which anything on the outside corner of the specific quadrant is considered high and anything near the main intersection is considered mid-low (Figure 17.1). Here is a simple rundown of your placement in each quadrant and how we arrived at your profile:

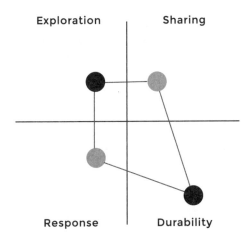

Figure 17.1 The Soldier

EXPLORATION

Soldiers score in the mid- to low range of this quadrant; it's all about what they believe is necessary within a presentation. You might not believe that presentation design is important, that practicing out loud is crucial, or that you need to fuss over the flow of your talk. But these aspects of your presentation are important, and they amplify your message. They are particularly powerful if you are comfortable with the message itself and you can easily discuss the main points at any time. Think of this quadrant as a gingerbread house: Sure, your message may be able to stand on its own without all of the candy decorations. But missing these elements defeats the core of what a gingerbread house really is—a beautiful celebration of practicality *and* sugar.

SHARING

Similar to Exploration, Soldiers score in the mid- to low range of Sharing. There could be many different reasons that you fumble with onstage delivery. Maybe you feel self-conscious about your own ability, and you hope that the message will speak for itself. Maybe you are uncomfortable telling stories or including humor in your talk. Either way, a great vision deserves a vibrant speaker who will sell the concept to the audience. Your delivery is critical to its success, and it is almost as important as the message itself.

RESPONSE

Your perspective about networking and response might be summed up with the question, "Why stick around to answer questions when I can direct people to a website?" Soldiers score in the low range of Response, and it could be due to (spoiler alert!) their high score in Durability. They are inspired to create online platforms such as blogs or websites to project their message when they can't. Soldiers miss a key opportunity when they avoid Q&As and group activities. Those are the moments when audience minds can change and long-term personal connections can be made.

DURABILITY

This is the quadrant where Soldiers march to victory, scoring in the high range. This all comes down to the selection of your message and your desire to see the world change for the better. You crave a large, diverse audience and seek the biggest stage possible. This is where the digital age aids your quest, providing a way for you to project onto personal computers and smartphones around the world. Soldiers know that originality is key, as well as the timelessness of their message. Consider the difference between a speaker talking about a dieting fad and a nutritionist discussing general wellness: a Soldier would lean toward the age-old wisdom of the nutritionist rather than jumping on board the latest trend.

SPOTTING A SOLDIER IN THE WILD

Meet Hannah, a political activist and volunteer in her community. She is intelligent, optimistic, and excited to see positive change for her city and the country at large. Her focus is on education and the money currently allocated to local schools to pay for supplies. It's simply not enough. Every day, students share textbooks, and teachers use the last drop from every dry-erase marker in the district.

Because of her passion and because she has seen firsthand the effects of school budget cuts in her own community, Hannah has decided to run for district leader during this election year. She has everything she needs to launch her campaign: enthusiasm, a great-looking website, and a transparent set of goals so that constituents will know exactly what she stands for.

Hannah has already begun filling her website with information and printing yard signs and banners. Her energy is boundless. She avoids coffee and instead is fueled by ambition and the vision of a brighter future for local students.

In two weeks, she is scheduled to announce her candidacy at a community event. She wants her speech to be short, about 10 minutes, and to touch on all of the most important initiatives of her campaign. Even without preparation, Hannah knows what she wants to say. There are so many aspects about her community that she loves and wants to improve.

The problem is that Hannah is so focused on the cause that she is forgetting to mold herself as an ideal champion for it. Her delivery is unrehearsed and uneven, jumping from topic to topic as quickly as her mind travels. Because her speech is only 10 minutes long, her call to action should be more than just "Vote for me." It should be an invitation for further discussion after the meeting is finished. Overall, she needs to polish her style from start to finish to become a credible, authentic, and clear choice for the community. There's more to politics than policy. It's about personality and the way a candidate relates to his or her potential voters.

Soldiers are like a pair of binoculars. Their range of vision stretches far into the distance, but the scope of the view is narrow. Hannah might not like the idea of changing her style or including a personal story, but this much more relatable approach will help her build supporters and become more memorable.

YOUR NATURAL HABITAT

A big message deserves a big crowd. While Soldiers may not be comfortable onstage or even in front of a small group, they are usually emboldened by the importance of their message and can deliver. What is comfort to a Soldier?

If you have a significant message that is meant to last, then aim to deliver it to as many people as possible. Use webinars, social media streams, and other digital megaphones to help you in the journey. You probably already have a few of these strategies in place, so branch out to the real world. Invite people you know to an event, or upgrade the size of your venue. If you're presenting at work, for instance, use the larger conference room, and invite people from other departments to hear you speak. And if they aren't sure why they were invited, lure them in with free doughnuts. Whatever it takes to make your voice heard.

BRAWN (STRENGTHS)

Driven

World changing

Lasting

You succeed in a category where many other personas stumble, which is in delivering a message that has a long-lasting effect across a wide variety of audiences. Even when challenged to make a business pitch or an educational presentation, Soldiers are able to turn the message into one that breaks boundaries and could have enough momentum to change the world.

Soldiers are also experts at building personal brand platforms for themselves. They know the importance of a great-looking website and the reach a viral message can have. Their ability to create messages that last by using modern tech gives them an edge that's hard for other personas to match.

TRAPS (WEAKNESSES)

Detached

Obsessed

Uncritical

It's the little stuff that brings down a Soldier's performance. A single-minded focus on the message alone won't make you well rehearsed, great onstage, or connected to your audience. In fact, it can undermine the credibility of your argument and even cause you to seem dull or detached from your audience. That's where practice and mindfulness of your audience's needs come in handy, which can be accomplished only when you do your homework.

As mentioned earlier, Soldiers also struggle with the idea of "gingerbread" decor as adding value to a presentation. Soldiers need to keep in mind that good presentation design is beautiful *and* supportive of the message. Stories and, yes, even jokes can be helpful as well. These additions appeal to audiences who are also looking to be entertained.

YOUR NATURAL ALLY

Want to learn how to improve your overall message and performance on stage? Take a page from the Educator playbook (Chapter 10) and connect with that persona to complement your skills.

YOUR PREY

A Soldier's message appeals to those who like reading self-improvement books and articles and are eager to see change in themselves and the world around them. Other Soldiers make the perfect target, in fact, as well as Creators and Scholars. Thankfully, your prey won't worry about your organization or delivery as long as the message is meaningful and potent.

YOUR PREDATORS

A message can't look you in the eyes, shake your hand, and ask how your kids are doing. If you rely on message alone, then you won't make a human connection with the personalities who need more from interactions. This includes Liberators, Educators, and other audience members who look for the heart of a story. Win them over by personalizing your message, making sure you show them how it changed you specifically and why you're standing in front of them today.

FIVE DOS AND DON'TS

DOS

1. Split your preparation time among the following actions: researching your message to find supporting data, working on your storyboard and deck design, and rehearsing your entire presentation out loud at least six to eight times.

2. Let your audience see a more human side to your message by sharing a personal story at the beginning or end of your talk.

3. There's so much more to a presentation than the final call to action. Consider the last time you were moved by a speech in a movie or a real-life event, and take note. What did the presenter do that you can emulate?

4. Pay special attention to your audience's expressions during the course of your talk. When do they look most interested? When are they about to fall asleep? Use this information to refine your delivery and practice more audience mindfulness going forward.

5. Yes, you have a world-changing message to deliver. But your audience is still going to need an answer to that age-old question: "What's in it for me?"

DON'TS

1. Don't neglect to share the research or proof points that made you such an advocate of your cause. Ask yourself this question: "What persuaded me to become a Soldier for this?"

2. Don't forget to use body language to express your passion about the subject. Move around! Wave your arms! You will feel more relaxed

as you move around freely, and your audience will feel the same way watching you.

3. Don't let your audience hear the final call to action in your speech without their knowing exactly how it will affect their own lives in a very personal way.

4. Don't lose sight of your presentation goals. You need to convince your audience that your large vision can be achieved by taking baby steps that start "today."

5. Don't underestimate the power of discussion with your audience. Let them take the floor at the end of your talk to ask questions or offer comments about the message itself.

THE IDEAL SOLDIER

There is no such thing as a bad persona. There are only areas to improve on within your range of strengths and weaknesses. With that in mind, what do ideal Soldiers look like?

1. They bump up their preparation time to enhance presentation design, refine their storytelling, and rehearse until they're comfortable.

2. They take a step back from their long-term vision and focus on addressing immediate audience needs. What are their audience's hopes, fears, and concerns?

3. They create a personal brand that is worthy of their vision, offering their expertise and inviting discussion through all platforms.

Let's revisit the tale of Hannah, our up-and-coming politician with some great ideas and plenty of zeal for her cause. What happens when she refines her skills and works to become an ideal Soldier?

1. She dedicates time to rehearsing her talk at the community center, starting with a story about local kids and peppering the talk with personal anecdotes.

2. She offers to speak with anyone who has questions after her presentation, and she stays to mingle and network with the audience.

3. She develops a personal brand as a vehicle to share her excitement with others, putting more information about herself and her causes on the Internet.

It may not feel natural to position yourself as a salesperson for your own cause, but you need to add that extra layer of personality to succeed. Ideal Soldiers come equipped with a message that they feel passionate about, but they are also open to incorporating those extra touches that make their audience's experience special. Be a Soldier whose tactics support his or her overall strategy. Your message deserves no less.

PART II

THE

4

QUADRANTS

Chapter 18

BE YOUR BEST
BADGE PROFILE

ongratulations! You now have a Badge. Own it. Embrace it. Be proud of it. You have a presentation persona that only a tiny percentage of the world shares, so you can consider yourself part of a unique group of individuals.

Get Your Badge! (JPEG):
http://ethos3.com/treats/yourbadge

How do you see yourself if you've never looked in a mirror? This book is like a mirror for you, and the simple fact that you have a copy in your hands gives you a competitive edge. Use this new dose of self-awareness to push the envelope, to test the edges, and to get a bit uncomfortable. Growth comes only from discomfort, but that discomfort at least lets you know where you can devote your energy.

LESSONS FROM A LOBSTER

While perusing YouTube recently, I (Scott) was reminded of a great interview with Dr. Abraham Twerski on the topic of discomfort and stress. He uses the life of a lobster as his metaphor, and it is absolutely amazing.

Here's an excerpt from the piece:

I came across an article "How Do Lobsters Grow?" that whetted my curiosity. How do lobsters grow? After all, lobsters are soft animals that live inside a rigid, inflexible shell. How can they grow?

The article explained that as a lobster grows, the rigid shell becomes very confining, and it feels oppressed. The lobster then hides under a rock formation to protect it from predatory fish and sheds its shell. It then produces a larger, more spacious shell in which it feels comfortable.

However, as the lobster grows, this new shell eventually becomes too confining and oppressive, so the lobster repeats the process. Off with the restricting shell, producing a more spacious one. This process is repeated until the lobster reaches its maximum size.

So much for the article, but the lesson is that it is the discomfort that causes the lobster to shed the oppressive shell and allows it to grow. Just think what would happen if a lobster had access to a doctor! It would complain of discomfort and get a pill to relieve it. With the discomfort gone, the lobster would never shed its shell and would not grow, dying as a tiny lobster![1]

Growth isn't possible without pressure and painful discomfort. It may not always be pleasant, but it's necessary if we are to improve.

We encourage you to continue challenging yourself to push harder, experiment more, keep what works, and drop what doesn't. If you were disappointed by one of your scores, we encourage you to embrace it as an opportunity to grow. Ask yourself how this newfound knowledge can help you improve and master your skills. We want you to really question how you can manage those vulnerabilities and weaknesses and maybe even turn them into strengths temporarily. The reason we say "temporarily" is that we believe you are who you are. Can you change? Absolutely. But, in the beginning, it will be short term. Statistically speaking, you will eventually migrate back to being the person you are at your core, and that is perfectly fine because your score is based on learned skill sets, or presentation habits, if you will. Just as you can break a bad habit, you can also grow in a quadrant if you are willing to make a proactive change. If you want to improve a quadrant score for a certain big talk or important keynote, you can do it, temporarily.

Long-lasting growth takes persistent and sustained practice. If you want to work on three or four quadrants, that can be done as well. It will just take a bigger reinvention.

DON'T BE AFRAID TO REINVENT YOURSELF

You may find yourself with an opportunity to reinvent yourself right now. According to investor and author James Altucher, a reinvention of one-self takes about five years.[2] It may be faster. It may be slower. However, should you feel the need to do so, migrating from one profile to another is going to take disciplined work.

Don't be afraid to change. Change is good. Change is healthy. Change will push you to be a better you.

The good news is that you can change. You aren't locked into one specific persona. If the Liberator profile is ultimately where you want to be, you can get there with intention and hard work. If the Scholar profile is more attractive and a better fit for your personal brand, then work toward it. If the Activator profile appears to be what your supervisor and organization need, put in the effort. It is absolutely doable.

LET'S GET SCIENTIFIC

If you are ready to grow or maybe even change, you'll enjoy the final chapters in this book. They are loaded with tips and tricks to help you modify and adjust if you want to truly excel at the art and science of public speaking. Dive into the intricacies of the four quadrants in greater detail and find prescriptive information that should leave you feeling more empowered and in control of your destiny as a presenter.

Chapter 19

QUADRANT 1: EXPLORATION

E verything starts with curiosity. It's the curious mind that begins the journey. It's the curious mind that craves new information. It's the curious mind that explores and prospers.

It's this same curious mind that makes some of today's best presenters. They dig. They grind. They succeed. They have an explorer's heart.

WHY EXPLORATION MATTERS WITH PRESENTERS

Your score in Exploration determines how you approach your presentation assignments. Are you naturally curious? Do you do the hard stuff: research, content creation, innovative design, narrative sculpting, and preparation? For a minority, this comes easily because they love it. However, for most presenters, Exploration is one of the most difficult components of any presentation. It requires patience and diligence.

EXAMINING A PROFESSIONAL FROM THE PAST

The year was 1940, and Britain was just one big loss away from being defeated by Germany. They were battling on the beaches of Dunkirk, and everything was looking very dim for the British troops. However, in a surprising turn of events, British troops were able to evacuate, avoiding defeat and a potential withdrawal from World War II. This was an unexpected surprise and remarkable success given that only 45,000 British troops were expected to be rescued off the beaches of Dunkirk, but 338,000 were saved,[1] keeping Britain in the war with a fighting chance. Following this amazing event, on June 4, 1940, Winston Churchill delivered his "We Will Fight on the Beaches" speech to fuel the newfound enthusiasm of his battered country. Here is an excerpt from that incredible speech:

> We shall go on to the end, we shall fight in France, we shall fight on the seas and oceans, we shall fight with growing confidence and growing strength in the air, we shall defend our Island, whatever the cost may be, we shall fight on the beaches, we shall fight on the landing grounds, we shall fight in the fields and in the streets, we shall fight in the hills; we shall never surrender, and even if, which I do not for a moment believe, this Island or a large part of it were subjugated and starving, then our Empire beyond the seas, armed and guarded by the British Fleet, would carry on the struggle, until, in God's good time, the New World, with all its power and might, steps forth to the rescue and the liberation of the old.[2]

He delivered this specific section of the speech in 61 seconds, and he said the words "we shall" a total of 10 times, which is a testament to his intention to unite his country. Churchill understood the importance of Exploration by choosing his words wisely and practicing repetition to rally his people behind such a significant cause. This is a technique used by some of today's most prominent speakers. The human brain loves to have information repeated.

LEARNING FROM A PROFESSIONAL TODAY

In July 2009 in Oxford, England, Daniel Pink opened his TED Talk "The Puzzle of Motivation"[3] with a confession. It started like this:

I need to make a confession at the outset here. A little over 20 years ago, I did something that I regret, something that I'm not particularly proud of. Something that, in many ways, I wish no one will ever know, but here I feel kind of obliged to reveal. In the late 1980s, in a moment of youthful indiscretion, I went to law school.

Pink utilized an entire 40 seconds of his 18-minute talk simply to weave a veil of mystery that he then followed with a creative punch line. It's funny. It's engaging. It's incredibly powerful. His talk continues with some brilliant points about business and motivation, including citing research from experts such as these:

- **Psychologist Karl Duncker and his candle problem.** "So, ladies and gentlemen of the jury, take a look at this. This is called the candle problem. Some of you might know it. It was created in 1945 by a psychologist named Karl Duncker. He created this experiment that is used in many other experiments in behavioral science. And here's how it works. Suppose I'm the experimenter. I bring you into a room. I give you a candle, some thumbtacks, and some matches. And I say to you, 'Your job is to attach the candle to the wall so the wax doesn't drip onto the table.' Now what would you do?"

- **Professor Sam Glucksberg and the power of incentives.** "I want to tell you about an experiment using the candle problem, done by a scientist named Sam Glucksberg, who is now at Princeton University, U.S. This shows the power of incentives."

- **Economist Dan Ariely and the study of rewards.** "Let me give you an example. Let me marshal the evidence here. I'm not telling a story. I'm making a case. Ladies and gentlemen of the jury, some evidence: Dan Ariely, one of the great economists of our time, he and three colleagues did a study of some MIT students. They gave these MIT students a bunch of games, games that involved creativity, and motor skills, and concentration. And they offered them, for performance, three levels of rewards: small reward, medium reward, large reward. If you do really well, you get the large reward, on down."

It's one example after the next. As with all presentations by Daniel Pink, everything is research backed, data driven, well planned, and delivered with passion, humor, and enthusiasm. This TED Talk alone is evidence that he takes the process of researching, exploring, and planning his presentations very seriously. He's knowledgeable, scripted, and definitely well rehearsed. He has mastered the quadrant of Exploration.

MASTERING THE EXPLORATION QUADRANT

The world was in love with their iPhones. Sales were going through the roof.[4] But Apple decided to take it one step further. On January 27, 2010, Apple introduced the world to the iPad. A 54-year-old Steve Jobs took the stage and started with this opening statement:

> We want to kick off 2010 by introducing a
> truly magical and revolutionary product today.[5]

What's immensely beautiful about this line was that he was beginning the process of building up to reveal the iPad. But the audience didn't actually get to see the device until the nine-minute mark. What he did here was threefold. He (1) painted a magnificent vision, (2) withheld revealing the actual iPad as a way to build anticipation, and when that was at its peak, (3) finally made the incredible reveal. It was a highly deliberate and intentional way to tackle the presentation.

It was a regular practice of Steve Jobs. According to Matt Drance,[6] a former Apple developer, "I worked at one point for 72 sleepless hours for something that Steve Jobs showed onstage for nine seconds."

This level of planning and rehearsal is part of the Apple DNA because of Steve Jobs.

OBSESS ABOUT YOUR CONTENT

One of our favorite authors is Steven Pressfield. He's written a number of great books on creativity, art, doing the hard thing, and facing what he calls "resistance." One of our favorite quotes is from *The War of Art*:

> Resistance plays for keeps. It aims to kill.

As you move forward, you need to look at presentations in three parts:

1. Content

2. Design

3. Delivery

Content is the most important, but it is also the least sexy of the three areas. This component makes up a majority of the Exploration quadrant. If you are intimidated by this umbrella, then we have a very easy suggestion for you.

The best presentations embrace the Rule of Three. Just think about it. Aristotle taught that the best presenters should have ethos (character), pathos (passion), and logos (logic or evidence).[7] He also encouraged the idea of having a beginning, middle, and end. Building from that same logic, you should have only three points because the human brain works like this: 1, 2, 3, . . . I forget.

Let's take this one step further. If you want to start embracing the Rule of Three, then we have a format for you. And here is the fun fact. It's a format you already know. Tell them what you are going to say. Say it. And tell them what you just said. You have heard this many times, but you'll be amazed by how few people actually apply it. If we want to put it in a business context, it can be broken down into the following Five Presentation Stages.

Stage 1. Tease

The climate. State or tease the current market or cultural situation.

The problem. What problem do your customers have?

The solution. How is your product or service the solution to this problem? How are you serving a purpose or making meaning?

Stage 2. Unveil the Mystery

The reason. In 10 seconds or less, state why everyone is here to hear you speak.

The preview. What are your three main points?

Stage 3. Inform and Ignite

Point 1. Main point with at least three supporting proofs.

Point 2. Main point with at least three supporting proofs.

Point 3. Main point with at least three supporting proofs.

Stage 4. Lock It Down

The review. Review your three points.

Stage 5. Launch

Call to action. What is the next step? What do you want the audience to do?

Tell them what you are going to say. Say it. Tell them what you just said. It's that simple.

Here are some additional resources to guide you on the right path:

A Storyboard Template (pdf):
http://ethos3.com/treats/storyboardtemplate

A Story Development Template (pdf):
http://ethos3.com/treat/storydevelopmenttemplate

As you begin to craft your message using this format, please be mindful of the following tips.

KEEP IT SIMPLE

The best presenters speak at roughly a fifth- or fourth-grade level, as can be measured using the Flesch-Kincaid grade-level readability formula. Looking at today's business or political scenes, Bill Gates typically speaks at an eleventh-grade level,[8] Steve Jobs spoke at a fifth-grade level,[9] Hillary Clinton speaks at an eighth-grade level,[10] and Donald Trump speaks at a fourth-grade level.[11] Jobs and Trump are typically known as speakers who are easy to understand and remember because of the simplicity of their content. If you want to accomplish the same feat, then you need to use language a fifth grader would understand. Avoid acronyms, internal jargon, and long sentences.

The Power of Simplicity (Video):
http://ethos3.com/treats/simplicity

KEEP IT CLEAR

Let's say you are visiting a new city, and you are about to give a talk. You decide to engage the audience early with a quick question regarding a local morning news event. Here's the question you throw out there: "A car was getting chased by cops this morning. Did you see it?" That's not a clear statement. One person is thinking of a blue car; another, a red one. One imagines a Mustang; another, a Lamborghini. Others are wondering if this event was related to the sirens they heard this morning on their side of town. Sure, it's great for your audience's imagination, but the message isn't clear.

According to a study by Jonathan Schooler of the University of California, Santa Barbara,[12] our brains wander up to 30 percent of the time, and that number can be as high as 70 percent when we're engaged in routine activities such as driving. Your audience's minds are already naturally prone to wander, so do the heavy lifting for them and provide the details. Here is how you can approach that opening line: "A red Toyota Corolla was getting chased by cops this morning on I-40 West. Did you see it on TV?"

KEEP IT SHORT

We're big fans of Daniel Pink. You may have already picked up on that because we cited him as an example earlier. We love his research, his innovative thinking, and how he approaches presentations. Pink has gone on record as saying that the very best presentations are about "brevity, levity, and repetition."[13]

The best presentations are short. They are to the point. And they repeat the important points. If your meeting organizer says you have 60 minutes to give your next talk and you have practiced and rehearsed and you are at 49 minutes, then you are at 49 minutes. Don't add 11 minutes of fluff. Better still, use the remaining time for a Q&A or discussion.

CARE ABOUT YOUR DESIGN

Every presenter is looking for that extra edge, especially when it relates to presentation design. But before you open up a tutorial in Photoshop or take a PowerPoint course online, you need to understand one critical element: *cognitive load theory*.[14]

Cognitive load theory (CLT) posits that our working memory is limited, that our brains can absorb only so much information when new ideas are shared or presented to us, which is our total cognitive load. This load is made up of three demands: *intrinsic*, *extraneous*, and *germane* (Figure 19.1).

> **The intrinsic load (level of difficulty).** Have you ever noticed that some content is easy to learn while other subject matter is difficult? For instance, adding and subtracting may be easy, but calculus feels a bit more complex. That's because calculus has a higher intrinsic load. Your responsibility as a presenter is always to keep it simple so your content is memorable.

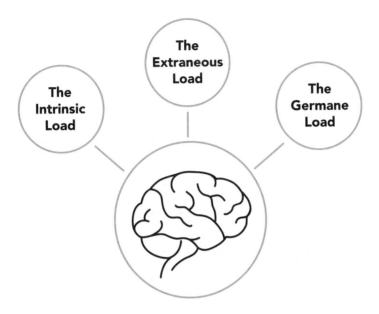

Figure 19.1 The Three Demands on Our Cognitive Load

Presentation design tip. When including charts and diagrams, break them down into bite-size pieces by utilizing build and transition slides to show how everything comes together.

The extraneous load (how information is presented). The good news with the extraneous load is that you have full control as a presenter. How you present will dictate how intense this load is on your audience. For instance, you can use a whiteboard and draw a circle for your audience, or you can verbalize what a circle looks like, which would be more difficult for your audience to process.

Presentation design tip. When describing something, capitalize on the opportunity to draw, use photos, or showcase anything visual.

The germane load (the building blocks). Don't judge me (Scott), but when I eat chicken nuggets or ramen soup, I think of my mom. No joke. These were among my favorite meals as a kid, and my mom obliged, probably because they were cheap, fast, and easy.

My brain associates these food items with my mom because of my experiences. The connections, processes, and building blocks that take place in our brains to develop a certain level of expertise is the germane load.

Presentation design tip. Make sure your choice of content and imagery connects the dots for your viewer. You can ensure this by opting for visual storytelling. Anything that provides context will help the learning process.

Remember, the human brain can take in only so much information. Aim for simplicity and your message will be remembered.

START BY REMOVING THE BULLETS

Did you know that the human brain processes visual information 60,000 times faster[15] than text-based information (aka bullet points)? In fact, information retention increases by 42 percent[16] when using visuals instead of text. So it should come as no surprise that we are not huge fans of bullet points. In fact, we strongly feel that bullets are like bullets—they will kill your presentation.

The Power of Visuals (Infographic):
http://ethos3.com/treats/visuals

Let's look at the sample slide about Brian in Figure 19.2. It would take me 7 to 10 seconds to share this slide with an audience. It's boring. It's predictable. There is nothing sexy about it.

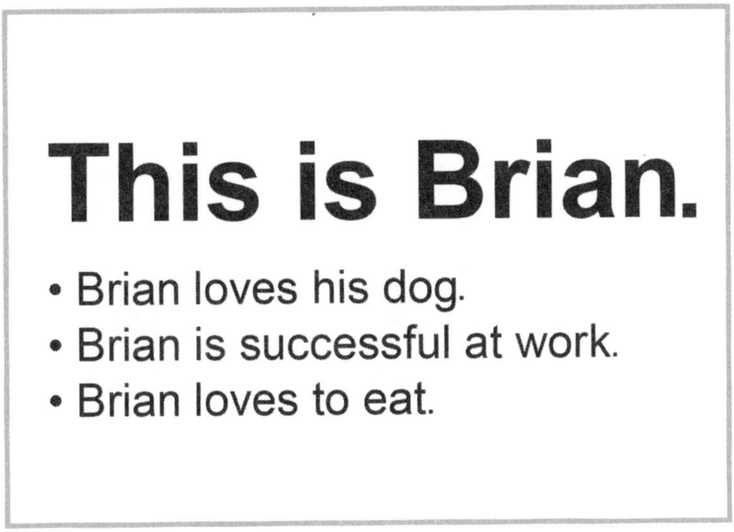

This is Brian.
• Brian loves his dog.
• Brian is successful at work.
• Brian loves to eat.

Figure 19.2 A Single Slide About Brian

What if we stretched this out onto four separate slides? It still would take only 7 to 10 seconds to present, but it would also be far more visually engaging, as can be seen in Figure 19.3. See the radical difference? Get rid of those bullet points.

This is Brian.
Brian loves his dog.
Brian is successful.
Brian loves to eat.

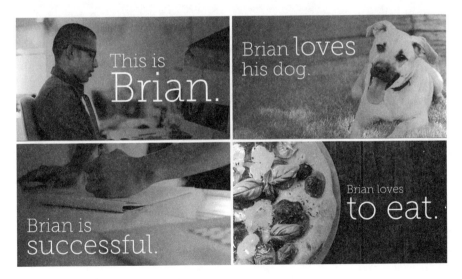

Figure 19.3 Four Slides About Brian

CHOOSE PHOTOGRAPHY

You've probably heard the Chinese proverb that a picture is worth a thousand words. This couldn't be more true for the presentation space. Visuals matter. We hope we are now on the same page about bullet points, so let's discuss the alternative: photography with typography.

As much as we don't want you to use bullet points, we want you to avoid templates whenever possible. Granted, templates are required for certain organizations when you need to keep consistency across departments or teams, but whenever a presentation is fully in your control, we suggest you stay away. Let's look at the example in Figures 19.4a, 19.4b, and 19.4c.

Figure 19.4a Changing Your City

Figure 19.4b Changing Your Life

Figure 19.4c Changing Your World

In the figure, we are seeing three slides from a random presentation. Each slide consists of a photo with large text. It's not a template, but the slides are unified by their look and feel. It's a much more visually engaging option compared with the alternative.

RESPECT YOUR TYPOGRAPHY

Today, everyone is a typographer. If you have access to a keyboard and a basic software program, you have control over typography. If you craft e-mails, write for a blog, or build presentations, you have control over typography your great-grandfathers would envy. Be thankful. Typography was an art form available only to the ink-stained laborers of the early nineteenth century. A lot has changed since the days of Gutenberg, but the sad reality is that even though today's presenters have control over type, they don't quite understand it as an art form. Let's change that right now.

How to Choose Fonts for Presentations (Infographic): http://ethos3.com/treats/fonts

We have established that removing bullets is essential and using photography and typography will add value. Here's how you can take it one step further. Opt for better fonts.

You need to know the difference between serif and sans serif fonts (Figure 19.5). *Serif fonts* have protruding edges, while *sans serif fonts* are without those edges, and they work very well in digital platforms such as presentations. Use sans serif fonts in your next presentation. You may mix and match them, but make your primary font a sans serif.

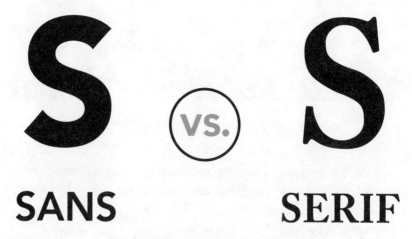

Figure 19.5 Serif and Sans Serif Fonts

PUT EVERYTHING INTO PRACTICE

We've covered a lot in this section: the cognitive load theory, eliminating bullets, photography, and typography. Let's put all of this new information into practice with a story of a presentation makeover that transformed a beast into a beauty.

A few years ago, we worked with our good friends at DNN Software (shout-out to Dennis Shiao for making this happen). As with most businesses, DNN Software was struggling with the classic Death by PowerPoint symptoms: bullets, headers, lots of text, a logo on the corner of every slide—all the usual stumbling blocks. It didn't matter what content they inserted into the template. The effect was simply "eh." They teamed up with Ethos3 because they wanted to move past that feeling.

Enter the slide makeover. DNN Software's original deck was 22 slides. What you are now going to see is the redesign of 3 of those original 22 slides. Let's have a look!

Figure 19.6 Example 1: Before

The "eh." This was an ordinary, run-of-the mill title slide. It included the title of the presentation, the presenter's name and job title, and the company's logo. It was all very forgettable because of the lack of visual appeal.

Figure 19.7 Example 1: After

The solution. We simplified the message by focusing on the title and letting that be the core idea. It was clear. It was pretty. And it was to the point, which meant that it would probably be remembered.

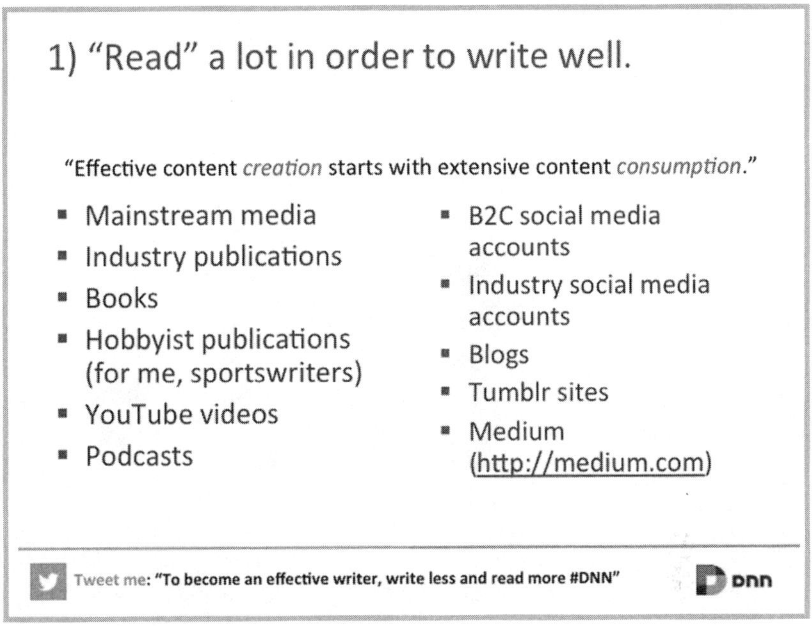

Figure 19.8 Example 2: Before

The "eh." The main problem here was the hearty abuse of bullet points. It contained 11 points in one place, making it difficult to retain any of the content. Yikes!

Figure 19.9 Example 2: After

The solution. Why not simplify the amount of text and complement that with an image? The human brain retains visual information more quickly than text-based information, so anything that encourages this learning style is a huge improvement over pure text.

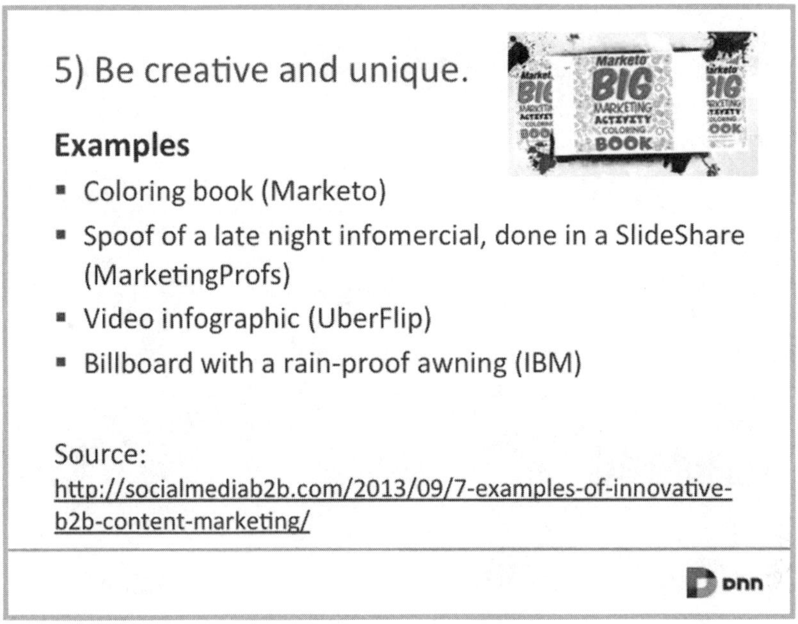

5) Be creative and unique.

Examples

- Coloring book (Marketo)
- Spoof of a late night infomercial, done in a SlideShare (MarketingProfs)
- Video infographic (UberFlip)
- Billboard with a rain-proof awning (IBM)

Source:
http://socialmediab2b.com/2013/09/7-examples-of-innovative-b2b-content-marketing/

D ᴅɴɴ

Figure 19.10 Example 3: Before

The "eh." There was too much going on here. We had a header, a big image callout, bullets, and a website address at the bottom. What was the audience meant to focus on? It was a mystery made for Sherlock Holmes.

Figure 19.11 Example 3: After, Slide 1

Figure 19.12 Example 3: After, Slide 2

The solution. We split this into two slides. On slide 1, we focused on the original header and paired it with an image. On slide 2, we featured some examples.

If the "before" DNN slides look familiar to you, don't fret! A presentation makeover is still possible, even for slides much scarier and with many more bullet points. They just require a heightened sense of awareness and a willingness to part with your old ways.

REHEARSE AND KEEP ON REHEARSING

Once you nail down your content and design, you need to embrace the mindset that every presentation requires a number of rehearsals. If your boss wants you to present on an unfamiliar subject matter, it requires a minimum of 7 to 8 rehearsals. Growing up, I had a pastor who practiced his sermon 30 times before Sunday. Ultimately, it's about finding the right balance for you. If you think practicing your presentation twice the night before and once the morning of your talk will make you succeed, you are dead wrong.

In 1981, Jerry Seinfeld practiced 200 times[17] for his five-minute comedy bit on *The Tonight Show with Johnny Carson*. Like Seinfeld, most comedians are obsessed not only with their number of rehearsals but with the quality of their material as well. Does this task come easy for them? Absolutely not. Just imagine how many jokes were written, tested, and filed away, never to be used again, when Seinfeld was preparing for his *Tonight Show* appearance—and that was before the rehearsal even started.

Rehearse. That's it. There is no secret or magic formula for this one. Get in front of a mirror. Get in front of a camera. Get in front of a room of your friends or family. Just make sure you rehearse. Rinse and repeat. No excuses. Keep practicing.

CONCLUSION

Exploration is the strong, concrete-filled foundation of all great presentations. It's difficult to master. Rightly so, because it is the most important of the four quadrants. All are essential, but if you made us pick one that really matters, it's this one, so don't neglect it. Instead, embrace it, and continue to perfect it.

REMEMBER

- Distill your next presentation down to three points.

- Use the Five Presentation Stages to outline your next talk.

- Respect the cognitive load theory.

- Eliminate bullet points.

- Use photography with typography on your slides.

- Choose sans serif over serif fonts when designing your presentation deck.

- Rehearse seven to eight times before every presentation.

Chapter 20

QUADRANT 2: SHARING

deas are transmitted every single day. Upon further examination, most are distributed via facts and stats, while the best are expressed creatively through stories, visuals, and great delivery.

Research shows that a compelling story makes all the difference with audiences: 63 percent of presentation attendees remember stories, while only 5 percent remember statistics.[1] When a story is delivered by a dynamic speaker, you are in for a treat. It's what the Sharing quadrant is all about.

The Five Beats of Storytelling (Infographic):
http:ethos3.com/treats/storytelling

WHY SHARING MATTERS FOR PRESENTERS

Your Badge score in Sharing illustrates how you perform and deliver your message (oratory and visual) onstage. Are you charismatic, confident, conversational, comfortable with your hands and feet, and dressed appropriately for the venue? Do your slides look gorgeous, or were they built using the latest PowerPoint template? It's everything that comes to mind when you think about the very act of delivering a talk. It's your voice, your nonverbal behavior, and everything else you do onstage.

EXAMINING A PROFESSIONAL FROM THE PAST

In the 1950s, the world was introduced to a trailblazing businesswoman who was decades ahead of her time. She took a struggling product and made it into a huge success by utilizing her charismatic public speaking skills in a "party plan" system she created. Her name was Brownie Wise, and the product was Tupperware, which sold over $2 million worth of products[2] in one calendar year. In a short period of time she created a plastic food-storage empire that was adored by households across America for many years.

Brownie Wise did not inherit success. She worked for it. In the 1940s, she found herself divorced single mom. At that time, a Stanley Home Products dealer came to her door, and according to Bob Keating,[3] author of *Tupperware Unsealed*, this person fumbled the presentation. Wise thought, "I could do better than that." The rest is history. Wise soon took a position with Stanley, and eventually she made her way to working with Earl Tupper of Tupperware.

How did Wise take a failing product and make it a household name? It was her ability to present and sell. She had the gift of being able to woo anyone she came in contact with because of her magnetic personality, depth of knowledge, and passion for what she was selling. Wise understood the importance of the Sharing quadrant. She was electric and a great storyteller, and she made every home party appear effortless and easy. Her ability to lead, inspire, and rally ushered women into the workforce to make their own money and help provide for their families. She is a heroine with Durability.

LEARNING FROM A PROFESSIONAL TODAY

In February 2012 in Long Beach, California, writer and lecturer Susan Cain delivered an amazing TED Talk, "The Power of Introverts,"[4] which was based on the brilliant research she did for her book *Quiet*.

There were many components that made her research and her talk brilliant, but the special item worth noting for this discussion was her use of a particular prop: a briefcase. She held this briefcase the entire first minute of her 18-minute talk as she painted a picture of her self going off to summer camp at the age of nine with more of a desire to read books than to make new friends. You can't help but relate to her story as you are flooded with your own memories of going to camp or traveling.

Throughout her talk, she used this prop to tell a beautiful story with precision and well-rehearsed punch lines. It was clear that every word she shared was carefully chosen and every action was rehearsed and planned. The end result? Her audience fell in love with her story and her research. Cain mastered the Exploration quadrant in order to shine in the Sharing quadrant. She told a beautiful story, she made her content relatable by incorporating a prop, and she used gestures and nonverbal behavior to enhance audience interaction and feedback.

MASTERING THE SHARING QUADRANT

If you are an entrepreneur or just passionate about business in general, then the name Gary Vaynerchuk is probably familiar. You may have read one of his books, or perhaps you subscribe to his YouTube channel. The guy loves video, and he is brilliant at connecting with his audience 24/7. He's completely magnetic and passionate, and it comes through every time he takes the stage or records a video.

Gary Vaynerchuk rose to popularity via his *Wine Library* TV show, and he really struck it big with his exuberant 2008 Web 2.0 Expo keynote,[5] where he said the following:

> If you love ALF, do an ALF blog. If you collect Smurfs,
> Smurf it up. Whatever you need to do, do it!

But Vaynerchuk struck a chord about three and a half minutes into his talk when he knelt down onstage and pleaded with his audience to stop complaining and step up. This small move made him relatable and tore down any potential walls between him and the audience.

Vaynerchuk shocked the world with his unique speaking style, brutal honesty, and authentic approach. For his presentation at HubSpot's 2012 INBOUND conference, he dropped a whopping 76 f-bombs in

45 minutes and used only one PowerPoint slide. That's unheard of in today's business climate, but it didn't matter. Why? He knows how to work the stage and speak from the heart. He did it so well that it earned him a standing ovation that morning. Vaynerchuk doesn't rely on technology or fancy gimmicks. He just wants to share what's in his heart and on his mind.

A sharing heart is at the core of all great presenters. They care about adding value. They care about giving back. They care about making mental and emotional deposits that will make a radical difference in the lives of their audience. In other words, great presenters know how to maximize their moment on stage because they are masters at sharing their message.

BEING PROACTIVE RATHER THAN REACTIVE

Let's face it. We live in a world full of judges. For every presentation you give between now and the day you retire, you are going to be judged by every single person. What we want to do now is provide you with some tips and tricks to minimize the level of judgment you will face.

DRESS THE PART

We have two rules of thumb:

1. DRESS ACCORDING TO YOUR OBJECTIVE.
If you want to raise $2.7 million for your startup, then dress the way someone would dress if he or she were asking for $2.7 million.

2. DRESS ACCORDING TO YOUR BRAND.
If you work for a stuffy and stodgy corporate brand, then dress in stuffy and stodgy clothes. If you work at a hip and cool agency, then dress in hip and cool clothes. That also applies to your personal platform. If you

are known as being innovative and cutting edge, then dress in innovative and cutting-edge clothes.

When in doubt, overdress for your presentation, and treat it with the same level of seriousness you would a job interview. If you play the conservative card, then we suggest being mindful of the following items:

Shoes. Black or brown shoes are your best bet. They are safe and traditional, and they don't raise any eyebrows.

Ties. If you opt for a tie, go with solid colors and nothing too bright or abstract.

Jewelry and Makeup. Sometimes makeup or a certain piece of jewelry can be a distraction. Tone it down. You can't go wrong with a string of pearls or a simple gold chain. When in doubt about a piece, don't wear it.

HAVE A BACKUP PLAN

We're going to borrow from our friend Guy Kawasaki on this one. In his book *The Art of the Start*, he says that everything that goes wrong during your presentation is your fault. It's true. If the projector dies, it is your fault. If your laptop dies, it is your fault. If the batteries in your remote die, it is your fault. Everything with your presentation is your responsibility, so you need to plan and prepare accordingly.

Start by showing up on time. If you are invited to speak at a location you have never been to before, arrive 45 to 60 minutes early to scope out the room and check the setup. Will you be presenting via a 16:9 format? 4:3? Whiteboard? You must be prepared. Upon your arrival, make sure that you have two to three backup plans. Is your presentation also saved in Dropbox? Do you have it on a flash drive? Do you have a copy of it ready to go on your iPhone or Android device? We live in the era of the cloud and mobile devices, so excuses or technological errors are unacceptable.

Remember, Murphy's law is real: "Anything that can go wrong, will go wrong." We mention it only because we see it happen all the time. A lack of a backup plan will find a way to reveal itself in the ugliest situations. Don't be the next victim.

PERFECT THE REFLECTION

When you present, everything you do and everything you share is a reflection on you. It always amazes us when we see someone who has obviously spent hours creating and designing a beautiful presentation slide deck only to give us a plain-looking handout in Microsoft Word. It's an instant credibility killer, and it is a poor reflection on the presenter. Aim for consistent quality among all the assets you will share and deliver.

If you treated your Exploration quadrant seriously, then we hope you have a beautiful-looking slide deck. Just remember that if it looks cheap, you look cheap. If it looks amateurish, you look amateurish. Everything you say and display is a direct reflection on you.

ACHIEVING AUTHENTICITY

One of your main goals as a presenter is to be authentic. Simply, you need to be yourself when you are in front of a roomful of people or at center stage. We have all had our fair share of experiences as audience members, and we know how easy it is to spot a poser or faker. Embrace some of the following rules.

GET HONEST FEEDBACK

The best place to understand how others perceive you and your level of authenticity is to start with something like a 360 review. And here is the really exciting news: you can use Badge to do peer reviews of your presentation style just like a traditional 360 review. Simply have your colleagues take the assessment on your behalf. The traditional 360 review is a practice we take very seriously at Ethos3, where we give every team member an opportunity to assess his or her peers and colleagues by submitting a review of them. We'll evaluate everything from leadership skills to job knowledge to how they live our core values. This same level of seriousness can also be applied to the Badge assessment, which makes it an excellent 360 tool.

SELF-DISCLOSE INTELLIGENTLY

According to a *Harvard Business Review* article,[6] stories are great at building on your relationships with others. They are not great at starting those relationships. I (Scott) will give you a recent example from my own life. My wife and I were invited to dinner by some friends we had just met. Over the course of the evening, the conversation shifted toward hobbies and exercise. One person divulged his love of weight lifting and his hatred of cardio, specifically running. He then asked, "What sport do you participate in?" I shyly answered, "Well, I'm a triathlete. I love to swim, bike, and run." Obviously, this was not a big deal to me or him, but it is a great example of how an individual can reveal too much too soon. Be careful not to share too much until you learn more about your audience.

You have to pick and choose your moments to be vulnerable. Sharing information about yourself can help break down barriers, but when you share too much, it can quickly turn from helpful to awkward.

DON'T BE AFRAID

At the end of the day, you cannot be afraid to be yourself, warts and all. You were asked to speak at this engagement for a reason. The meeting organizer, prospect, or client obviously found you or your brand intriguing, so don't deviate from that foundation.

PRESENTING WITH PASSION

You can spend the rest of your career trying to master all the quadrants, but here is a simple reality: if you are not passionate about your message, no one else will be. We love these quotes:

The most powerful weapon on Earth is the human soul on fire.
—Ferdinand Foch

Light yourself on fire. You'll be amazed at the number of people who line up to watch you burn.
>—*Rob Roy,* The Navy SEAL Art of War

Passion is everything.

EMBRACE YOUR POWER ZONES

Harvard professor and researcher Amy Cuddy delivered the beautiful TED talk "Your Body Language Shapes Who You Are,"[7] in which she revealed how just two minutes of holding a power pose can increase levels of testosterone and lower levels of cortisol (the stress hormone).[8] While Dr. Cuddy's work has been challenged, we thought it worth sharing here.

MANAGE YOUR TOP HALF

To control and maximize this part of your body, you need to keep your head and chin up (Figure 20.1a). You may also complement this effort by putting your arms up in a V shape, which will give you the feeling of power and authority.

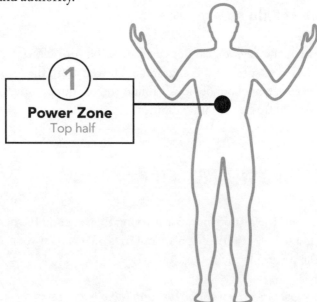

Figure 20.1a Power Zone: Your Top Half
Source: http://blog.ted.com/fake-it-til-you-become-it-amy-cuddys-power-poses-visualized/.

MANAGE YOUR BOTTOM HALF

Think about your feet and everything below your waist (Figure 20.1b). Do a Superman or Wonder Woman pose with your hands on your hips, legs apart, and chest out. It showcases control and power. When confronted by another—perhaps your boss is yelling at you—keep your legs apart, and it will display that you are not a pushover.

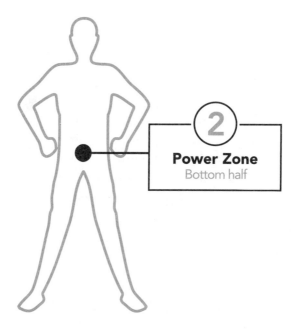

Figure 20.1b Power Zone: Your Bottom Half
Source: http://blog.ted.com/fake-it-til-you-become-it-amy-cuddys-power-poses-visualized/.

The Importance of Nonverbal Communication (Infographic): http://ethos3.com/treats/nonverbal

SPEAK WITH AUTHORITY

There are two speaking styles plaguing our business culture right now. The first is *uptalk* and the second is *vocal fry.* You need to avoid both.

Uptalk. Uptalk is the act of taking a statement and turning it into a question by using an upward inflection. It's so prevalent that some experts are beginning to call it an epidemic. If we stop and analyze a fictional conversation with a customer service representative, it may look like this example:

> *Customer service associate:* Whom am I speaking with?
>
> *David:* My name is David?
>
> *Customer service associate:* Date of birth?
>
> *David:* 4/19/84?

Even though David intended to sound confident, it can be easy for him—or anyone, for that matter—to get thrown off by a question and then answer it with a question rather than a confident statement. This behavior is often referred to as Valley Girl-speak; the presenter or speaker is perceived to be an airhead or ditz. This seriously undermines credibility.

Vocal Fry. Vocal fry is an equally troubling epidemic. It happens when an individual uses his or her lowest vocal register. Our vocal chords are composed of four registers.[9] The lowest is *fry*, followed by *modal*, *falsetto*, and *whistle*. Most people speak in the modal range. However, according to several recent studies,[10] many people are using vocal fry more often these days. In fact, two-thirds of women are using vocal fry on a regular basis. The more vocal fry, the less authority we project, so as presenters we need to take note.

How do you fix these issues?

1. LISTENING.
Listen to yourself and others, and focus on becoming more self-aware and mindful moving forward. Stop uptalk and vocal fry before they start.

2. BREATHING.
Make sure you connect your voice to your breath. Focus on letting your breath come from your belly when you speak.

BE A WORDSMITH

If you watch any Apple presentation, executives use a few select key words. You'll constantly hear words such as "great," "amazing," "wonderful," and "incredible." This is no accident; it is highly intentional. If we revisit the iPad launch presentation from 2010,[11] Figure 20.2 shows what Steve Jobs and his executive team's word count looked like.

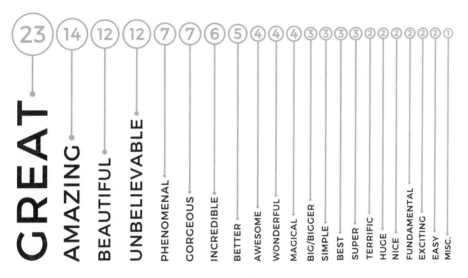

Figure 20.2 Steve Jobs and his executive team's Word Count in the 2010 iPad Launch Presentation

When you think of iPhones, Apple wants you to think "great" or "amazing." When you think Apple Watches, the company wants you to think "incredible." As presenters, we need to do the same thing. Pick a few key words, and make sure to drop them strategically throughout your next talk.

CONCLUSION

Mastering the Sharing quadrant is no easy feat. It takes confidence, charisma, and lots of preparation. It's hard to be magnetic onstage, but it is not impossible. Anyone can do it if he or she is willing to put in the time and effort. Be intentional with every word and action.

REMEMBER

- Dress according to your objective or brand.

- Show up early to your presentation and have multiple backup plans.

- Manage your fears and self-disclose intelligently.

- Present with passion.

- Embrace your power zones.

- Avoid uptalk and vocal fry.

- Be a wordsmith.

Chapter 21

QUADRANT 3: RESPONSE

A
t a very young age, we were all taught the importance of being kind and nice to others. Our parents insisted we use words such as "thank you" and "please." We were taught manners. We were taught humility. We were taught how to have a thankful heart and always think of others before ourselves.

But somehow, we began to lose this attitude of gratitude as we aged. There's the mortgage to pay, that deadline to meet, and that recital to attend. It's hard to feel grateful when there are so many demands on your life and your day.

The very act of presenting is no different. We expect people to show up. We expect them to listen. We expect them to appreciate us and our message. But that's not the reality. Audiences owe you nothing, and a mindset of entitlement rather than gratitude gets presenters in trouble.

> **The primary reason you should create and give a presentation is to provide value to your audience.**

Think about it. When you are planning to give a presentation, you are generally consumed with questions such as:

How do I simplify my content and data?

How do I incorporate videos into my presentation?

How do I come across as authentic?

How do I avoid being anxious or nervous onstage?

How should I dress for my presentation?

They all contain "I" and not "they." Your perspective needs to change.

WHY RESPONSE MATTERS FOR PRESENTERS

Your Badge score in Response showcases how you are received by your audience. Do they like you? Do they hate you? Do they think you are boring? Perhaps they think you are incredibly interesting. Response is also indicative of whether you prepare your message to appeal to your audience's hearts and minds.

EXAMINING A PROFESSIONAL FROM THE PAST

Just three days after the September 11, 2001, attacks on New York and Washington, President George W. Bush gave an electrifying speech via a bullhorn to the rescue workers at Ground Zero. It was a short and simple. Why was it so powerful?

His approach was a bit unexpected. The rescue workers couldn't hear him, and he responded with a few simple words that empowered the whole country.

Here's his entire speech:

President Bush

Thank you all. I want you all to know—it [the bullhorn] can't go any louder—I want you all to know that America today, America today is on bended knee, in prayer for the people whose lives were lost here, for the workers who work here, for the families who mourn. The nation stands with the good people of New York City and New Jersey and Connecticut as we mourn the loss of thousands of our citizens.

Rescue Worker

I can't hear you!

President Bush

I can hear you! I can hear you! The rest of the world hears you! And the people . . . and the people who knocked these buildings down will hear all of us soon!

Rescue Workers

[Chanting] U.S.A.! U.S.A.! U.S.A.! U.S.A.! U.S.A.! U.S.A.! U.S.A.! U.S.A.!

President Bush

The nation . . . the nation sends its love and compassion . . .

Rescue Worker

God bless America!

President Bush

. . . to everybody who is here. Thank you for your hard work. Thank you for makin' the nation proud, and may God bless America.

Rescue Workers

[Chanting] U.S.A.! U.S.A.! U.S.A.! U.S.A.![1]

America and the rest of the world changed that day. For the first time in a long while, Americans began to unite, and President Bush's approval rating skyrocketed to 90 percent, the highest ever in Gallup history.[2] That day, he understood that he needed to share a message that would inspire and grab the hearts of his audience. He needed to provide direction for a country in shock. He needed to make a lasting impact. He observed. He listened. He took action. It's what the people needed, and he provided it.

LEARNING FROM A PROFESSIONAL TODAY

One of my favorite presenters is Anthony Robbins. He's passionate. He's charismatic. He's knowledgeable. And he knows how to own a room even without PowerPoint. It's hard not to like him. Robbins coaches executives, athletes, world leaders, and even college students who are looking for that competitive edge. You may already be familiar with his very successful audio programs *Personal Power* and *Get the Edge*. He's been helping people for decades, and he continues to experience monumental success because audiences love him. He cares for them, and they, in turn, care for him.

Several years ago, Hanna, a suicidal 13-year-old girl, was attending one of his conferences with her parents. Robbins went to her and spent six minutes with her, doing one-on-one coaching, ultimately helping her achieve a major breakthrough. They concluded their time together with a giant hug. Through this effort, he was able to change the group, by changing one person.

If you have had the privilege of attending any of his *Date with Destiny* or *Business Mastery* courses, you'll know what I mean about Robbins's passion and love for his audiences. Anthony Robbins knows how to educate, motivate, and get anyone moving toward massive action. I have attended his goal-setting workshop (part of *Get the Edge*) for the past few years now, and I always leave feeling inspired and challenged to start taking small steps toward my objectives.

If there is one core element that holds true with any Anthony Robbins presentation or seminar, it is this: he has a very deep passion and love for his audience. At his core, he cares for people. He wants people to be happy and fulfilled and to achieve their goals and dreams. He'll do everything in his power to help people overcome their fears, grow, get financially stable, find love, be better parents, and maximize their lives.

Robbins understands the importance of the Response quadrant. His messages are always simple and actionable, which makes him memorable and magnetic. It's a wonderful combination.

MASTERING THE RESPONSE QUADRANT

The day was February 11, 1990, and the location was Cape Town, South Africa. On this day, Nelson Mandela was released from prison after serving 27 years behind bars. Twenty-seven years. There are some of you reading this right now who aren't 27 years old. That's a long time to spend in prison for trying to protect your country from an oppressive regime.

Despite the abuse, mistreatment, and unfairness, Mandela focused on his audience rather than himself when giving his speech shortly after being released. Here is a part of his opening:

> Friends, comrades, and fellow South Africans.
>
> I greet you all in the name of peace,
> democracy, and freedom for all.
>
> I stand here before you not as a prophet but as a humble servant of you, the people. Your tireless and heroic sacrifices have made it possible for me to be here today. I therefore place the remaining years of my life in your hands.
>
> On this day of my release, I extend my sincere and warmest gratitude to the millions of my compatriots and those in every corner of the globe who have campaigned tirelessly for my release.[3]

This short excerpt is a total of 99 words, 49 of which were about his audience. He continued his talk with "I salute" and "I pay tribute to" messages, which expressed his humility and service to others. How much of your next presentation is focused on your audience?

CARE ABOUT YOUR AUDIENCE

The primary reason you should create and give a presentation is to provide value to your audience. Plain and simple. The presentation is not about you. It's about them. Ask yourself these five questions when thinking about your audience.

THE FIVE QUESTIONS ABOUT YOUR AUDIENCE

1. WHO AM I ADDRESSING?

In every presentation environment you are going to find yourself facing a 50/50 balance of introverts and extroverts. That lesson was taught to me years ago by a dear friend and mentor. Here's how I was taught to distinguish the difference between the two. Imagine that you have a battery in the middle of your chest. If you are an extrovert, that battery stays energized when you are at dinner with friends, attending a party, or participating in any social event. The minute you begin to spend time by yourself, though, your battery begins to get depleted and you need to start socializing again to get it charged back up. Now, if you are an introvert, you are the exact opposite. The lesson: you can never lean in just one direction. For instance, if you are completely lecture-based, you will lose the attention of your extroverts. If you are entirely interactive, you will lose the attention of your introverts. You must respect both.

2. WHAT KEEPS THEM UP AT NIGHT?

I spent the first few years of my career working in the area of marketing. My days consisted of writing marketing plans and then executing the action plans. Day in and day out, this was my life. At this time in my marketing career, everything was about selling the features and benefits of our products. Fast-forward to today, and marketing is all about selling pain relief. The lesson: make sure your presentation is providing value and solving problems for your audience.

3. HOW CAN I MOLD MY CONTENT TO BEST REACH THEM?

According to a Stanford lecturer and expert, structured presentations are 40 percent more likely to be retained and remembered.[4] The lesson: craft your presentation so that it follows a logical flow and structure where you transition from every main point clearly. Use this format: What? So what? Now what? If you can follow this simple guideline, you'll be able to create a message that can break through barriers.

4. HOW CAN I GET THEM TO ENGAGE WITH ME?

Tell more stories. Here's a great Indian proverb: "Tell me a fact, and I'll remember. Tell me a truth, and I'll believe it. But if you tell me a story, I'll put it in my heart forever." Stories are how we connect and communicate as humans, so if your presentation is based solely on facts and stats, then your audience is going to react in one of two ways: (a) they will agree with you or (b) they will disagree with you. You don't want to risk the probability of reaction (b), so tell stories. If you tell a story, your audience won't agree or disagree, but they will engage with you. Think about it. When I (Scott) was 12 years old, I broke my arm. It was a nice spring day, and I was attempting to ride my bike down a gigantic hill in our neighborhood with no hands, and then BAM! I ran smack into a curb, flew off my bike, and went tumbling down the concrete sidewalk. Now, did you just agree or disagree with that very short story? I'm going to argue that you engaged instead. Maybe you broke your arm as a kid as well, or perhaps your child just broke his or her arm. You aren't agreeing or disagreeing. You are engaging.

5. WHAT DO I NEED THEM TO DO NEXT?

Every presentation needs a call to action. We'll repeat that. Every presentation needs a call to action. Your audience needs to know what you want them to do next. Are they supposed to buy something, download something, or read something? What are they supposed to do with the information you just presented? By providing a clear call to action, you are also providing a clear purpose and reason for your talk.

If you can't answer those questions with 100 percent confidence, then don't pass "Go," don't collect $200, and get back to the drawing board. Now, if you can answer those questions with full clarity, then you need to do the following.

CHANGE YOUR LANGUAGE

Most presentations today are all about the presenter and not the audience. Think about the last conference or presentation you attended where every slide was internally focused rather than externally focused. I'll give you an example. Remember that slide at the last meeting you attended on which the header said "Agenda" and it was followed by three to five bullet points? Don't remember? It probably looked like the slide in Figure 21.1.

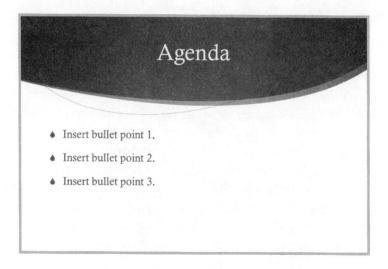

Figure 21.1 The Generic Conference Agenda Slide

Wouldn't it have been far better if the word "Agenda" had been re-placed with "How you can make an impact!" (Figure 21.2) or "Why this matters to you!" (Figure 21.3) or "How we can do this together!" (Figure 21.4). See the difference? The latter are about the audience. They utilize words such as "you" and "we."

Figure 21.2 Audience-Focused Slide: How You Can Make an Impact

Figure 21.3 Audience-Focused Slide: Why This Matters to You

Figure 21.4 Audience-Focused Slide: How We Can Do This Together

BE READY FOR MILLENNIALS

Your future audience will be composed of millennials. Are you ready?

As a generation Xer, I (Scott) grew up with Star Wars. It was the franchise of my time. You had a classic hero's journey of a *call to adventure*, followed by a *departure*, *initiation*, and *return* (Figure 21.5).

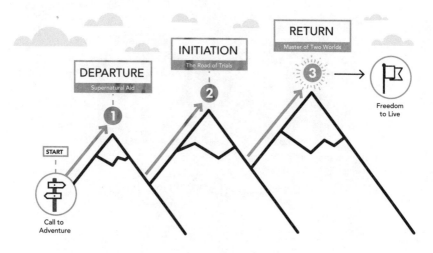

Figure 21.5 The Hero's Journey
Source: http://www.business2community.com/tech-gadgets/heros-journey -user-0814472#DW6LSE5XsJTXmtOI.97.

If you follow this sequence of events, it goes like this: Luke Skywalker is not happy as a moisture farmer on his home planet of Tatooine. He soon accepts a *call to adventure* in the form of Princess Leia's hologram message (*departure*). Luke soon finds himself entering an unknown world that is vastly different from anything he is comfortable with, which includes an eventual fight with the Empire and its intimidating Death Star. Luke continues to stifle the Empire's plan to rule the galaxy and is faced with an even larger dilemma: one of the Empire's fiercest leaders, Darth Vader, is his father, who he believes, at his core, is still good (*initiation*). As time progresses, Luke's gut eventually serves him well when his father decides to kill the Emperor, ruler of the Empire, which ultimately brings balance to the galaxy (*return*).

Star Wars was simple in design. It was the good guys versus the bad guys or light versus dark. It was a message that resonated with my generation. The same is true of Harry Potter and millennials, but here is the radical difference: unlike Star Wars, the Harry Potter franchise had some additional elements, five to be exact, as shown in Figure 21.6.

I want to call your attention to two of them: *teamwork* and *heroism*. Harry Potter is all about teams. You have House Gryffindor, House Slytherin, House Hufflepuff, and House Ravenclaw. In addition, Harry Potter

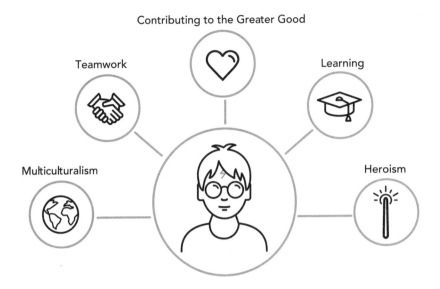

Figure 21.6 Harry Potter Franchise Thematic Elements
Source: http://www.millennialmarketing.com/2009/07/growing-up-with-harry-potter/.

was not gifted like Luke Skywalker was. In fact, he was average, but he was motivated by serving the greater good, which is exactly how millennials are wired today. Here's what this means:

Be purposeful. Make sure your next presentation serves the greater good. An easy way to accomplish this is by including the word "because." According to a recent Harvard study, when the word "because" was added to a presenter's call to action, participation jumped to 90 percent compared with 60 percent[5] when the word was not utilized.

Be social. Harry Potter was the first truly multimedia franchise. There were the books, movies, and toys, but also the Internet, which included trivia games, mugglecasts, puppet pals, and much more.[6] If any presenter expects to make a lasting impact, the presentation needs to live online and on multiple platforms for consumption and viewing.

Care about your audiences. Speak their language. Serve their needs and desires.

YOU MUST BE PERSUASIVE

If you want to strengthen your ability to persuade and influence, we recommend the work of Dr. Robert B. Cialdini,[7] who has written a number of great books on the subject. If you want a few tips and tricks, here's what we suggest (Figure 21.7).

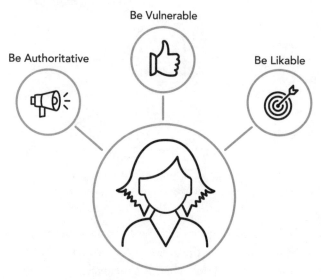

Figure 21.7 How to Be Persuasive

BE AUTHORITATIVE

Persuasion is a lot about having authority. From a presentation context, authority is best achieved when it comes from an outside source, so it is in your best interest to see if you can have someone introduce you before you take the stage. This will immediately earn you credibility and position you as the expert. If someone is not available to introduce you, see if you can have your credentials or bio highlighted in a brochure or one sheet that can be read before you begin your presentation.

BE VULNERABLE

We live in a transparent world. We're glued to social media on our phones, tablets, and desktops. People want an inside look at our lives, and presentations aren't much different. Don't be afraid to open up and share personal stories when appropriate. It will help tear down the walls between you and your audience and humanize you as a speaker.

BE LIKABLE

We like to think of being likable in the framework of two Ps: playful and polite. Audiences love those who know how to have fun with themselves and others, so showcase your playful side. Don't be afraid to make fun of yourself or display how you are a kid at heart. Assuming your parents did a great job of raising you, don't neglect to display your manners and be polite.

PLAN FOR UNPREDICTABILITY

No matter how much presenters prepare, they will never know exactly how an audience will react to their message. Will they love it? Will they hate it? The sad reality: audiences are unpredictable. They may be talkative. They may be tired. They may be inquisitive. They may even be hateful. Amazing presenters know how to control any situation, and that begins with knowing how to open and close your talk.

FIVE POWERFUL WAYS TO OPEN YOUR PRESENTATION

We all know that first impressions matter, so if you want to mitigate harsh or unnecessary judgment, you'll need to know how to open a presentation properly. Here are a few of our favorite tactics:

1. USE THE POWER OF SILENCE.

In February 2013, Amanda Palmer delivered a phenomenal TED Talk called the "The Art of Asking," and she opened with silence. She spent the first 18 seconds setting up her equipment and then being silent. By doing so, she built a confident stage presence. As viewers, we are left waiting and wondering what's next, putting all the power and authority in her hands. This is what makes it an amazing tactic. If you are feeling extremely confident and charismatic, it's definitely an approach worth adding to your toolbox.

2. LOOK TO THE FUTURE OR THE PAST.

Prospective and retrospective statements can be incredibly powerful when done right. I'll give you an example of each. Let's say you want to be *prospective* with your opening. If this is the case, you might want to open with a statement like this: "Ten years from now, mobile devices will be a thing of the past." Now you have the audience's attention. They are wondering how this can be. They love their iPhones. What could possibly replace them? No matter what they are wondering, you have them engaged from your opening line. Here's an example of a *retrospective* statement: "In 1969, we put a man on the moon. Today, we are beginning our journey to Mars." Again, it's a compelling statement that leaves your audience wanting more.

3. QUOTE SOMEONE.

I (Scott) am a big fan of Stephen Hawking. If I decide to open my next presentation with one of his quotes, it will automatically build my level of credibility. Let's see it in action: "Stephen Hawking once said, 'Intelligence is the ability to adapt to change.' That's exactly what I want to talk about with you today."

With a few words, I'm looking smarter than I actually am—just ask my wife.

4. SHARE SOMETHING EXTRAORDINARY.

Did you know that if you eat 30 to 90 grams of polar bear liver,[7] you could die? That's something extraordinary about something ordinary. As human beings, we love this type of information, so it is worth exploring as a potential presentation opener.

5. TELL A STORY.

Stories are part of our DNA. There are really no new stories. They are just retold in different ways by different people. Stories are forever. Open with one in your next presentation.

 Our Favorite Opening Method (Video):
http://ethos3.com/treats/opening

FIVE POWERFUL WAYS TO CLOSE YOUR PRESENTATION

Understanding how to open a presentation is critical, but knowing how to close one is just as important. Here are a few of our favorite techniques:

1. CIRCLE BACK AROUND.

Our favorite movies and books always circle back around. Two of our favorite directors are the Coen brothers. Their movies are a bit dark, incredibly introspective, and wildly popular. Their classic *Fargo* demonstrates this point. In the very first scene of the movie, you see a car driving on a snowy road. The movie's resolution concludes with a very similar image and tone. As an audience member, you are provided with a sense of closure, which has a powerful emotional impact.

2. BUILD UP TO SOMETHING.

Let's take another lesson from Hollywood. One film that stands out to me is Bryan Singer's 1995 hit *The Usual Suspects*. I won't reveal any spoilers. Suffice it to say that it ends with an amazing twist. Singer spends 106 minutes[9] building up to something very profound.

3. REPEAT THE IMPORTANT STUFF.

In 1999, neurobiologist Joe Tsien found that special communication channels in our nerve cells, called NMDA receptors, create new connections with associative (repetitive) learning. The protein GAP-43[10] makes nerve connections form quickly in response to repetition. So when Lincoln (we'll study him in just a bit) says "of the people, by the people, and for the people," it triggers our GAP-43 to make a new connection that we remember later. These connections are a recipe for a potent memory-boosting way to end your presentation.

4. MAKE A CALL TO ACTION.

Shockingly, 85 percent of sales pitches[11] fail to conclude with an ask for the actual sale. That's a disappointing statistic. Your audience has just invested 30, 60, or 90 minutes to hear you speak. It is imperative that you tell them what you want them to do next.

5. END WITH INSPIRATION.

Every human being loves a good pick-me-up, so if you can encourage your audience to take action—large or small—you have added true value to their lives. It's all about empowering your audience to take the next step, so close with hopeful and optimistic statements that will move them to action.

Our Favorite Closing Method (Video):
http://ethos3.com/treats/closing

MASTERING THE Q&A

If anything is going to get out of hand, it is going to be your Q&A. If you know your material, you are going to be in great shape. If you stumbled or failed somewhere during your talk, then be prepared for hecklers. Here are two ways to manage the troublemakers:

1. IGNORE THEM.

In his book *The Leader's Guide to Speaking with Presence*, John Baldoni talks about how the stage is your home and the audience are your guests. As long as you exude control, you should be in good shape. If the heckling is bad, unnecessary, or undeserved, then don't forget this principle: don't let them take over your house.

2. RESPECT THEM.

If there is something you need to work on, then work on it and become a better presenter because of it. You probably did mess up, and that is OK. Just fix it and learn from it for next time.

Owning the opening, close, and Q&A portion of your presentation will give you a radical competitive edge. You can control how others will perceive you when starting and ending your presentation. Experiment with a few techniques, and you'll soon find ones you love, and you'll deploy them frequently.

CONCLUSION

If you can master and dominate the Response quadrant, your audience will love you. The task is simple: make the presentation about them and not about you. If you approach your presentation through that lens, you won't go wrong.

 **REMEMBER**

- Make sure you can answer the five questions about your audience with confidence.

- Change your language and keep this in mind with every slide you create.

- Be ready for the millennials in your audience.

- To be persuasive, be authoritative, vulnerable, and likable.

- Choose a technique that works best for you when opening a presentation.

- Choose a technique that works best for you when closing a presentation.

Chapter 22

QUADRANT 4: DURABILITY

E very now and then, we are blessed with individuals who touch our souls, inspire us, challenge us, and change us—to be better, wiser, and stronger. They give us the rough kick in the butt we need to get going personally and professionally.

They have a long-term impact. We remember what they said during dinner the night after the talk, while we are driving to work a week after that, and for years afterward. They have what we like to call "presentation Durability."

Your audience is relying on you. Ben Franklin sums it up best:

> Without continual growth and progress, such words as *improvement*, *achievement*, and *success* have no meaning.

We must constantly be pushing ourselves to become better, to get outside our comfort zones, and to acquire new knowledge and skill sets so that we can make a lasting impact. The art of presenting is a complex task that requires constant refinement.

WHY DURABILITY MATTERS WITH PRESENTERS

Your Badge score in Durability showcases just how influential your message is on the lives of those who hear it. Are they moved? Think of some of the greats: Patrick Henry, Martin Luther King, Jr., and Susan B.

Anthony. These are the men and women who made a tremendous impact simply through the medium of presentation. There are countless others who make a powerful impact on others: coaches, counselors, teachers, and mentors. They change lives.

EXAMINING A PROFESSIONAL FROM THE PAST

July 1863. A special memorial was being held, and Edward Everett was the primary speaker for the day. In 1863, attention spans were not like the eight-second version[1] we have today. Audiences wanted long and lengthy talks, ones that would inspire and educate. Everett was considered a superstar orator, but his two-hour speech was not remembered by the 15,000 in attendance. Instead, the man who spoke right after him went down in history as delivering one of the best speeches of all time, one that lasted only two minutes (273 words). In fact, it was so short that there are no photographs of him onstage. He walked up, gave an absolutely dynamic presentation, and stepped down. Before photographers knew it, he was done, but lives were changed forever.

The man was Abraham Lincoln, and the speech was the Gettysburg Address.[2] Everett's speech is what brought people together, but it was Lincoln's speech that changed the world. What made this speech so enduring is that he didn't use flowery or archaic phrases. Instead, his words were short, simple, and concise—an approach he was recognized for during his time in office. The Gettysburg Address was not only simple, it was also incredibly moving. "A government of the people, by the people, for the people" was a beautiful way to describe the American experience, even in the wake of a tragedy.

At the time, people were talking about bringing slavery to an end. Lincoln used the Gettysburg Address to discuss equality. The notion that all men were created equal was radical for the period and completely revolutionary.

The Gettysburg Address is littered with simple and powerful statements, radical insights that changed an entire country. Lincoln exemplified the importance of the Durability quadrant; his message that day will be remembered forever.

LEARNING FROM A PROFESSIONAL TODAY

At the University of Texas (UT) at Austin, the graduating class of 2014 was honored with an amazing commencement address. The speaker that day was Navy Admiral William H. McRaven, ninth commander of the U.S. Special Operations Command. A heavily decorated Navy SEAL, he offered life lessons that were simple yet profound in a mere 20 minutes. Near the beginning of his talk,[3] he shared a line that was inspired by the university's slogan, "What starts here changes the world":

> Tonight, there are almost 8,000 students graduating from UT. That great paragon of analytical rigor, Ask.com, says that the average American will meet 10,000 people in his or her life-time. That's a lot of folks. But if every one of you changed the lives of just 10 people and each one of those folks changed the lives of another 10 people—just 10—then in five generations—125 years—the class of 2014 will have changed the lives of 800 million people.
>
> Eight hundred million people—think of it—over twice the population of the United States. Go one more generation and you can change the entire population of the world—8 billion people.

Immediately, he provided the purpose of his talk by highlighting that every person has value. He implied that all of us can make a big impact or perhaps even change the world. He then continued with 10 life lessons:

1. If you want to change the world, start off by making your bed.

2. If you want to change the world, find someone to help you paddle.

3. If you want to change the world, measure individuals by the size of their heart, not the size of their flippers.

4. If you want to change the world, get over being a sugar cookie and keep moving forward.

5. If you want to change the world, don't be afraid of the circuses.

6. If you want to change the world, sometimes you have to slide down the obstacle head first.

7. If you want to change the world, don't back down from the sharks.

8. If you want to change the world, you must be your very best in the darkest moment.

9. If you want to change the world, start singing when you're up to your neck in mud.

10. If you want to change the world, don't ever, ever ring the bell.

These life lessons are so very simple yet so very elegant. There is nothing fancy. Just honest insights that hit you in the gut and will resonate long after.

MASTERING THE DURABILITY QUADRANT

On September 18, 2007, a special group of folks got to witness in person one of the best presentations of the last 20 years. Randy Pausch, professor of science and human-computer animation, gave "The Last Lecture: Really Achieving Your Childhood Dreams"[4] at Carnegie Mellon University in Pittsburgh, Pennsylvania. It achieved further acclaim on YouTube, and it was ultimately published as a book of the same name in 2008 that became a *New York Times* bestseller.

In this presentation, Pausch discussed his life, his family, and his battle with pancreatic cancer. It's an emotional lecture filled with humor, great stories, many lessons, and nothing but relatable content.

He concluded his talk by making the following powerful and inspiring statements:

Brick walls let us show our dedication.

Don't bail; the best gold is at the bottom of the barrels of crap.

Be good at something. It makes you valuable.

Work hard.

If you do the right thing, good stuff has a way of happening.

The talk is littered with emotionally driven and powerful doses of wisdom that leave the audience wanting more. A connection like no other is made. The theme is simple: He's human. You are human. We are all going to die, but it is what we do between now and then that matters. He ended with an amazing statement:

The talk is not for you; it's for my kids.

It may sound selfish, but it actually achieved the opposite effect. It showed us where his heart truly was—with his children. Who can argue with someone wanting to be a great father? You can't. It's a truly inspiring lesson from someone who understood the power of Durability. His message was universal, and it will be remembered for years to come because it served his family—and the many.

DEVELOPING A UNIQUE POINT OF VIEW

When my wife and I (Scott) can't find a good show or movie on Netflix, our next-best alternative is to look for a stand-up comedy act. Our personal favorites include Ali Wong, Brian Regan, and Jim Gaffigan. Each has a unique style and persona—a unique point of view (Figure 22.1).

Figure 22.1 The Unique Style and Persona of Well-Known Comedians

As a presenter, you need to do the same. Develop your own perspective on life and the world around you.

Here are three suggestions to get you headed in the right direction:

1. DEDICATE THE TIME.

I'm a triathlete, but ice hockey is my favorite sport. For months, I had a terrible slap shot. Let's just say I'm glad you could hardly identify me with my helmet and mask. It was ugly. However, I wanted to get better, so I kept showing up. I kept swinging, and eventually, the puck started to lift off the ice. Eventually, it started to hit the net. In his book *Outliers*, Malcolm Gladwell discusses the "10,000-Hour Rule," which claims that the key to success is spending 10,000 hours on a specific task. If you want to be an expert, you must be willing to put in the hours.

2. FIND YOUR AUTHENTIC VOICE.

During the latter part of his career, my father worked for Anthony Robbins, so let's just say that success modeling was a big part of my life.

I love finding people who have done amazing things and studying how they accomplished so much. It's always intriguing to discover how they decoded the art of mastery. Now, it's great to model their methods, but it is dangerous to copy. Taking inspiration from another person is empowering, but becoming a "me too" of that individual is deadly. I'll leave you with this: it's better to be a collection of many than a duplicate of another.

3. FAIL AND FAIL AGAIN.

We love failure. Seriously. We absolutely love it. It is what makes us human. More important, it is what makes us better humans—if we learn from our failures and mistakes. There is nothing "overnight" about having a platform, so use every day to learn and fall flat on your face. Just make sure you get up again. So fail hard and fail fast. It's going to take an abundance of trial-and-error experimenting with visuals, gestures, and speaking styles that are unique to you—and that is perfectly OK.

Put in the time. Find your authentic voice. And don't be afraid to fail. If you are willing to do these things, you are on the right path to developing your own point of view.

BUILDING YOUR PLATFORM

You can have the best content, the prettiest deck, and the most amazing delivery style, but if you have no platform, you have no audience. The entire concept of Durability is about having a message that (1) will not only be loved and adored by others but (2) will also stand the test of time. You must have fans to help you embed your message and cement your legacy. First, you need to flex your muscles and prove that you're the expert. Here's how to hit the gym.

BECOME AN EXPERT

According to author and entrepreneur Tim Ferriss, anyone can become an expert in four weeks. That's it. It's completely doable if you are willing to put in the effort. Here are a few tips Ferriss suggests to accomplish this level of authority:

1. JOIN TWO TO THREE TRADE-RELATED ORGANIZATIONS WITH OFFICIAL-SOUNDING NAMES.

The main idea here is to associate yourself with the right industry labels. If you want a certain distinction, seek the title. For instance, if you just created a business, apply to become an LLC. Within a few days, you now have the name XYZ Company, LLC, which makes you look a lot more credible.

2. READ THREE TOP-SELLING BOOKS IN YOUR SPACE.

Ferriss says that if you read this type of material, you will know about 80 percent more than the standard person in that industry. I can attest to this fact as well. When I first started Ethos3, I consumed every book on presentations I could get my hands on.

3. WRITE A GUEST POST.

Piggyback on the success of others. If Johnny has 100,000 blog subscribers, then offer to write a guest post for him for free. Your content will be seen by 100,000 folks.[5]

These tips are easy to implement and deploy. It just requires some proactiveness on your part. If you start acting like an expert, people will soon see you as a thought leader.

PURSUE THOUGHT LEADERSHIP

You are probably reading this book right now because you are looking for ideas, concepts, and anything else that will give you a competitive edge. You are looking for leadership. People all over the world are doing the exact same thing as you. They are looking for knowledge. They are looking for wisdom. They are looking for smarter ways to do things. They crave fresh ideas.

Here's the good news. There is no better platform than a presentation for giving you the opportunity to showcase your expertise. Plan for it. Seize it. Own it:

Success occurs when opportunity meets preparation.
—Zig Ziglar

If you put in the hard work, you'll become a thought leader in your industry.

OBSESS ABOUT YOUR LEGACY

Achieving thought leadership is one thing. Securing a legacy is a completely separate challenge. I (Scott) don't know about you, but I really care deeply about my legacy. I want to leave something behind for those who are passionate about improving their presentation and public speaking skills. That fact alone is a big reason why I wrote this book. It's my small footprint in this world.

The good news is that we live in a world that obsesses about video. You can capture 4K video on the phone that is in your pocket. Everything you do can be recorded. When you pass away one day, what do you want to leave behind? Your presentations are a culmination of your greatest hits, so for starters, make sure you have something great to share.

RECYCLING YOUR DECK FOR MAXIMUM IMPACT

Here's what normally happens: A person gets tasked with creating a presentation. He or she creates it, shows up, presents it, and then files it away. People clap quietly, and then everyone leaves for lunch. That is a tremendous missed opportunity. Let's say your deck has 50 beautiful slides, some with amazing photography and typography and others with brilliant quotes, stats, and facts. All of that can be recycled for future endeavors. Specifically, they can be utilized as part of your content marketing efforts. Let's start with the basics.

A CASE STUDY

A few years ago Ethos3 had the privilege of working with the team at Buffer to revitalize one of their decks.[6] The Buffer team provided a deck called "Social Media Frequency," which had a ton of compelling statistics and details about how often publishers should post. It was rich with amazing content but lackluster in design. We spruced it up, gave it a visual facelift, and worked with their team to put it online. The first place it went was SlideShare. You can view the before slides in Figures 22.2a, 22.3a, and 22.4a and the after slides in Figures 22.2b, 22.3b, and 22.4b.

Figure 22.2a Social Media Frequency Slide: Before
Source: https://blog.slideshare.net/2014/06/30/slide-makeovers-buffers-social-media-guide.

Figure 22.2b Social Media Frequency Slide: After
Source: https://blog.slideshare.net/2014/06/30/slide-makeovers-buffers-social-media-guide.

Figure 22.3a Facebook: Post 5 to 10 Times per Week: Before
Source: https://blog.slideshare.net/2014/06/30/slide-makeovers-buffers-social-media-guide.

Figure 22.3b Facebook: Post 5 to 10 Times per Week: After
Source: https://blog.slideshare.net/2014/06/30/slide-makeovers-buffers-social-media-guide.

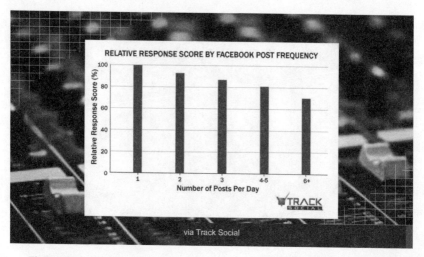

Figure 22.4a Relative Response Score by Facebook Post Frequency: Before
Source: https://blog.slideshare.net/2014/06/30/slide-makeovers-buffers-social-media-guide.

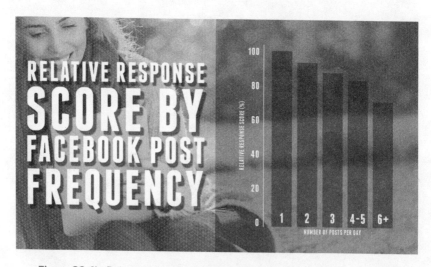

Figure 22.4b Relative Response Score by Facebook Post Frequency: After
Source: https://blog.slideshare.net/2014/06/30/slide-makeovers-buffers-social-media-guide.

If you are not familiar with SlideShare, it is the YouTube of Power-Point. If you have a deck, upload it to SlideShare, and voilà! You are now sharing your presentation with the rest of the world. At the time I was working with Buffer, I was writing regularly for SlideShare, so the slide deck was quickly turned into a blog post about the makeover process. I took a few select slides, as did Buffer, and shared them on Twitter, Facebook, and LinkedIn. Just like that we had maximum exposure across multiple channels.

Content Marketing with Presentations (Infographic): http://ethos3.com/treats/contentmarketing

According to recent studies, when content contains images, there is a probability that it will receive 94 percent more views than content without visuals.[7] In addition, visual content is 40 times more likely[8] to be shared on social media. Given that presentations, when done right, are entirely visual, success is inevitable. Plus, everything is measurable.

MEASURE YOUR SUCCESS

Once you have done the hard work, take joy in knowing that all your efforts can be measured. Total views. Check. Traffic sources. Check. Social actions. Check. Your content marketing strategy is a beautiful thing.

Presentations should always be part of any marketing strategy not only because they create the ability for the success of the strategy to be measured but also because they can increase your ranking across all browsers.

GET RANKED

A strong organic search presence is what every great marketer desires. Sites such as SlideShare, which has over 60 million users,[9] make organic search easy because they are incredibly search friendly. SlideShare will automatically transcribe the copy from your presentation, making it one of the Internet's most accessible websites, and search sites such as Google love it. The lesson: build presentation content around the search terms that your business dominates, and you will win.

33 SlideShare Tips (Infographic):
http://ethos3.com/treats/slidesharetips

CONCLUSION

This is a highly coveted quadrant because it is all about legacy. Mastery of Durability means that you build, design, and deliver presentations that stand the test of time. It is the predictor of your long-term success and value. It's tough to achieve, but it is also the most rewarding.

REMEMBER

- Try to create unexpected moments.

- Develop your own point of view.

- Work on becoming an expert.

- Build a platform and become a thought leader.

- Care about your legacy.

- Recycle your presentation and use it across social media channels.

Chapter 23

INTO THE WILD

Y ou did it. You are about to be set free back into the wild. We hope you enjoyed the journey as much as we did. But this is just the beginning. You have a new perspective, new paradigms, and an entirely new approach to presenting. We are so excited for you to begin this next phase. Be sure to wear your Badge proudly.

WORDS OF WISDOM

Before we go our separate ways, we want to leave you with some parting words. On January 20, 1961, John F. Kennedy delivered his famous inaugural address to the American public and the entire world. In this speech, he challenged every citizen to do the following:

> Ask not what your country can do for you—
>
> ask what you can do for your country.[1]

He understood that greatness comes from helping the many. Greatness is measured in service, not status. It's about how many you serve, not how many serve you. If you can find a way to serve the many, you'll find the path to greatness.

Focus on giving rather than taking. Care about your audience more than yourself. Your Badge is meaningless if you don't have the right mindset. Here's the reality we all face as presenters: the more people you affect, the more successful you will be. Develop a servant's heart and you'll see your speaking career light up.

Presenting is hard work. Period. It takes dedication and hours of practice behind the scenes. The good news is that you now have a competitive edge. Your Badge provides self-awareness. It gives you valuable weight that your peers are lacking.

The next step is your responsibility. Take this newfound knowledge and get better. Continue working on this beautiful craft that we call "presenting." The best place to start is with a stop-doing list.

CREATE A PRESENTATION STOP-DOING LIST

If you need a jolt of inspiration to get started on your personal journey, we suggest creating a stop-doing list for your presentations. One of my (Scott) end-of-year rituals includes creating two stop-doing lists, one for my personal life and the other for my professional life.

It's both deeply rewarding and humbling. You are confronted with bad habits you are too ashamed to admit you have. This task forces you to put them down on paper. It's difficult, but I never regret it. Within just a few minutes, I am pinpointing major flaws and behaviors.

Here's why I recommend that you do the same as you think about your professional career. Day to day, you are rewarded for what you initiate and achieve—but never for what you stop doing:

- You're praised for arriving on time for work, not for stopping being late.

- You're praised for being more productive on the clock, not for stopping your water-cooler talk.

- You're praised for meeting your deadlines, not for stopping your procrastination.

This system of action and reward might be the wrong way to approach it. Here's an example of what I mean.

Let's say you want to be a better presenter this year. You're tired of being nervous onstage, tired of putting people to sleep, tired of getting the same old results every time. You might tackle this resolution with a to-do list that looks something like this:

1. Go to bed early the night before my next presentation.

2. Rehearse seven to eight times in front of a family member or colleague.

3. Focus on presentation design.

4. Read one new presentation or public speaking book a month.

5. Seek professional training.

6. Go to a seminar once a quarter.

7. Model myself after successful presenters around me.

It's a beautiful vision, but the reality of maintaining the actions on this list may last only a week or maybe a month. The reality is that you will eventually find yourself burned out and not doing any of the above after a certain length of time. Consider all of those ambitious New Year's resolutions that appear and disappear like bubbles. We keep making them, but they keep popping. Here's a better solution:

> **Stop shortcutting my presentations.**

It's much easier to stop doing one thing than it is to start doing seven new things. Think about it. The choice to become a better presenter by taking seven actions sounds much more daunting than just deciding to stop shortcutting your presentations. Assuming you abide by it, it means you aren't going to shortcut your research, you aren't going to shortcut your rehearsal time, you aren't going to shortcut your design, and the list goes on and on. It means you will care more and stop taking shortcuts. Your presentation stop-doing list may be only one five-word statement, and that's perfect. The goal is to get it on paper so that you can keep yourself accountable. Don't make any more excuses.

A Stop-Doing List (pdf):
http://ethos3.com/treats/stopdoinglist

STOP MAKING EXCUSES

Most people are full of excuses. They're like a piñata, spilling out new excuses whenever they feel like life has dealt them a blow. "I didn't close that deal because the client just didn't understand." "I didn't get that promotion because my boss is a jerk." Or "I failed to deliver a great presentation because we don't have a design department." Enough already. The excuses need to stop.

We want you to acknowledge that there are no shortcuts, magic pills, or secret formulas. The best presenters have worked hard behind the scenes; there is no such thing as an overnight success in the world of presenting.

THE REST IS UP TO YOU

You have now been exposed to a plethora of content, 16 unique profiles, and a deep dive into presentation personas. Congrats on finishing the book. It has been an absolute pleasure joining you on this adventure of self-discovery. The self-discovery doesn't have to end here, and the future is looking really bright.

We would love to hear from you. Give us a shout-out. Say hello. Shoot us an e-mail at badge@ethos3.com so we can connect. We love presentations, and we would be happy to talk personas or presentation strategy with you any day of the week. Heck, if you want to talk craft beer with Sunday or triathlons with Scott, we would welcome those conversations as well. We're honored to be part of this journey with you, and we hope to meet you someday.

We've advised. We've coached. We've shared our best tips and tricks to empower you as a presenter. The rest is up to you. Take your Badge and own it. We'll see you out there in the wild.

Appendix

EXTRA TREATS

Not ready to leave yet? We aren't either. It's hard to say good-bye.

Now, who doesn't love a good treat? For those of you looking for something extra, we have put together a few items for you. This appendix includes some answers to frequently asked questions as well as access to all the links covered in this book and some new ones. Enjoy, and please don't forget to stay in touch.

FREQUENTLY ASKED QUESTIONS

1. Can I change my profile?
Think of the Badge assessment as step 1 in your presentation journey. Your profile should reflect your existing strengths, weaknesses, and aspects of your personality as it applies to speaking. Those are the tools you came equipped with. You can't change the profile you started with, but you can take steps to improve in each quadrant and become a better version of you. For example, if you love researching a topic but have a hard time onstage, your love of research won't die just because you become a more zesty presenter.

2. Which profile is the strongest? Which one is the weakest?
We know that one of the profiles (ahem, Liberator) scores in the mid- to high area of each quadrant. But sometimes this simply means that Liberators know how they *should* answer, but they don't necessarily put it into practice. A similar fact is true for profiles that score in the mid- to low

range of most quadrants: they might not be experienced presenters, and they aren't familiar with common speaking wisdom yet. We believe that everyone can improve. *Everyone*. Learning to be more critical of your skills and struggles is essential to becoming a better speaker.

3. What if I don't like my results?

If you're looking down at the list of weaknesses and shaking your head, don't panic! It's not going to be a perfect mirror image of what you struggle with onstage or off. If you feel like the profile doesn't appeal to you, focus on your score in each quadrant instead. Everyone is different. And everyone can improve.

4. What if I've never given a presentation before? Can I still take the test?

Yes! Our assessment is word associative, and it features a sample story at the beginning of the test for this reason. Many aspects of presenting may appear in other areas of your life, such as rehearsing for a best man's speech or interacting with others. You should be able to take the test and gain valuable insight even if the last time you stood in front of a group of people was during a fifth-grade book report.

5. Should I retake the assessment?

Once should be enough. After you've learned the best way to approach preparation, delivery, and audience interaction, your answers may change. The Badge assessment works best with your existing knowledge, and it is meant to take a temperature reading of your existing strengths and weaknesses. Once you know your starting point, it's up to you to improve your skills accordingly. There's no real reason to aim for a different profile once you improve. Thus, you won't need to take it more than once.

RESOURCES BUILT JUST FOR YOU

Looking for more? We've got you covered. Here's everything you need to complement your copy of *What's Your Presentation Persona?*

Chapter 1

Introduction to Badge (Video). http://ethos3.com/treats/introduction

Profile Cheat Sheet (pdf). http://ethos3.com/treats/cheatsheet

How to Do the 4 × 4 Breathing Technique (Video). http://ethos3.com /treats/4x4

Chapter 2
The Activator Spotlight (Video). http://ethos3.com/treats/activator

Chapter 3
The Advocator Spotlight (Video). http://ethos3.com/treats/advocator

Chapter 4
The Befriender Spotlight (Video). http://ethos3.com/treats/befriender

Chapter 5
The Captivator Spotlight (Video). http://ethos3.com/treats/captivator

Chapter 6
The Creator Spotlight (Video). http://ethos3.com/treats/creator

Chapter 7
The Curator Spotlight (Video). http://ethos3.com/treats/curator

Chapter 8
The Demonstrator Spotlight (Video). http://ethos3.com/treats /demonstrator

Chapter 9
The Director Spotlight (Video). http://ethos3.com/treats/director

Chapter 10
The Educator Spotlight (Video). http://ethos3.com/treats/educator

Chapter 11
The Liberator Spotlight (Video). http://ethos3.com/treats/liberator

Chapter 12

The Navigator Spotlight (Video). http://ethos3.com/treats/navigator

Chapter 13

The Performer Spotlight (Video). http://ethos3.com/treats/performer

Chapter 14

The Producer Spotlight (Video). http://ethos3.com/treats/producer

Chapter 15

The Scholar Spotlight (Video). http://ethos3.com/treats/scholar

Chapter 16

The Scientist Spotlight (Video). http://ethos3.com/treats/scientist

Chapter 17

The Soldier Spotlight (Video). http://ethos3.com/treats/soldier

Chapter 18

Get Your Badge (JPEG). http://ethos3.com/treats/yourbadge

Chapter 19

A Storyboard Template (pdf). http://ethos3.com/treats/storyboardtemplate

A Story Development Template (pdf). http://ethos3.com/treats/storydevelopmenttemplate

How to Choose Fonts for Presentations (Infographic). http://ethos3.com/treats/fonts

The Power of Simplicity (Video). http://ethos3.com/treats/simplicity

The Power of Visuals (Infographic). http://ethos3.com/treats/visuals

Chapter 20

The Five Beats of Storytelling (Infographic). http:ethos3.com/treats/storytelling

The Importance of Nonverbal Communication (Infographic).
http://ethos3.com/treats/nonverbal

Chapter 21

Our Favorite Opening Method (Video). http://ethos3.com/treats
/opening

Our Favorite Closing Method (Video). http://ethos3.com/treats
/closing

Chapter 22

Content Marketing with Presentations (Infographic). http://ethos3
.com/treats/contentmarketing

33 SlideShare Tips (Infographic). http://ethos3.com/treats
/slidesharetips

Chapter 23

A Stop-Doing List (pdf). http://ethos3.com/treats/stopdoinglist

Extras

Meet the Authors (Videos). http://ethos3.com/treats/authors

Free eBook: 99 Things You Didn't Learn About Presentations in School
(pdf). http://ethos3.com/treats/ebook

Need Help Sprucing up a Presentation? (pdf). http://ethos3.com
/treats/presentationdesign

Need Presentation Training? (pdf). http://ethos3.com/treats
/presentationtraining

NOTES

Introduction

1. https://www.washingtonpost.com/posteverything/wp/2015/05/26/powerpoint-should-be-banned-this-powerpoint-presentation-explains-why/.

Chapter 1

1. http://onresilience.com/2011/06/02/tactical-breathing-can-stop-stress-on-the-spot/.
2. http://99u.com/articles/19568/the-4-ways-you-can-use-body-language-to-your-advantage.
3. http://www.tandfonline.com/doi/abs/10.1080/01690960802159929?journalCode=plcp20&#.V5pBuJOAOko.
4. http://www.doctoroz.com/blog/janine-driver/3-body-language-health-secrets-revealed-whats-your-body-trying-tell-you-about-you.
5. http://www.businessinsider.com/grit-is-more-important-than-iq-2013-5.

Chapter 18

1. https://www.youtube.com/watch?v=3aDXM5H-Fuw.
2. http://www.jamesaltucher.com/2013/12/the-ultimate-cheat-sheet-for-reinventing-yourself-2/.

Chapter 19

1. http://www.express.co.uk/news/world/578885/Dunkirk-evacuation-World-War-Two-Germany-Britain.
2. http://historynewsnetwork.org/article/157508.
3. http://www.ted.com/talks/dan_pink_on_motivation?language=en.
4. https://www.apple.com/pr/library/2010/10/18Apple-Reports-Fourth-Quarter-Results.html.
5. http://everystevejobsvideo.com/original-ipad-introduction-apple-special-event-2010/.
6. https://www.quora.com/History-of-Apple-Inc-How-did-Steve-Jobs-prepare-and-design-his-keynotes.
7. http://www.european-rhetoric.com/ethos-pathos-logos-modes-persuasion-aristotle/.
8. http://blog.seattlepi.com/microsoft/2007/01/14/bill-gates-and-steve-jobs-keynote-text-analysis/.
9. Ibid.
10. http://www.huffingtonpost.com/entry/trump-speeches-reading-level_us_56e9899fe4b0b25c9184183f.
11. Ibid.
12. https://www.psychologytoday.com/blog/brain-wise/201301/our-minds-wander-least-30-percent-the-time.
13. https://www.youtube.com/watch?v=CUDqN7MNsRw.
14. https://elearningindustry.com/cognitive-load-theory-and-instructional-design.
15. http://blog.hubspot.com/blog/tabid/6307/bid/33423/19-Reasons-You-Should-Include-Visual-Content-in-Your-Marketing-Data.aspx#sm.00000k3rixxv99cnlrkxj94gno6a1.
16. http://www.slideshare.net/ethos3/your-business-needsvisualcontentinfographicbyethos3-30810350.
17. http://www.nytimes.com/2012/12/23/magazine/jerry-seinfeld-intends-to-die-standing-up.html?_r=1.

Chapter 20

1. http://www.slideshare.net/cmignault/20-sales-stats-that-will-change-how-you-sell-34969448/11-After_a_presentation63_of_attendeesremember.
2. http://mentalfloss.com/article/59687/how-single-mom-created-plastic-food-storage-empire.
3. https://www.youtube.com/watch?v=KfqkUGNVHlw.
4. https://www.ted.com/talks/susan_cain_the_power_of_introverts?language=en.
5. https://www.youtube.com/watch?v=EhqZ0RU95d4.
6. https://hbr.org/2013/10/be-yourself-but-carefully.
7. https://www.ted.com/talks/amy_cuddy_your_body_language_shapes_who_you_are?language=en.
8. http://hbswk.hbs.edu/item/power-posing-fake-it-until-you-make-it.
9. https://en.wikipedia.org/wiki/Vocal_register#Vocal_fry_register.
10. http://www.theatlantic.com/business/archive/2014/05/employers-look-down-on-women-with-vocal-fry/371811/.
11. https://www.youtube.com/watch?v=1ZS8HqOGTbA.

Chapter 21

1. http://www.americanrhetoric.com/speeches/gwbush911groundzerobullhorn.htm.
2. http://www.gallup.com/poll/4924/bush-job-approval-highest-gallup-history.aspx.
3. http://www.bet.com/news/global/2013/12/05/transcript-nelson-mandelas-address-on-his-release-from-prison.html.
4. https://www.gsb.stanford.edu/insights/matt-abrahams-how-do-you-make-memorable-presentation.
5. http://psychologyformarketers.com/power-of-because/.
6. http://www.millenialmarketing.com/2009/07/growing-up-with-harry-potter/.
7. http://www.influenceatwork.com/wp-content/uploads/2012/02/E_Brand_principles.pdf.
8. http://www.thefactsite.com/2015/04/100-mind-blowing-facts.html.
9. http://www.imdb.com/title/tt0114814/?ref_=nv_sr_1.
10. http://biologywriter.com/on-science/articles/repetitionlearn/.
11. http://www.nasp.com/article/DA02C4CB-C52C/it-s-ok-to-ask-for-the-sale-really-it-s-ok.html.

Chapter 22

1. http://time.com/3858309/attention-spans-goldfish/.
2. http://history.howstuffworks.com/historical-events/gettysburg-address2.htm.
3. http://news.utexas.edu/2014/05/16/mcraven-urges-graduates-to-find-courage-to-change-the-world.
4. https://www.youtube.com/watch?v=ji5_MqicxSo.
5. Adapted from http://nichehacks.com/become-a-niche-expert/.
6. https://blog.slideshare.net/2014/06/30/slide-makeovers-buffers-social-media-guide.
7. http://blog.hubspot.com/marketing/visual-content-marketing-strategy#sm.00000wppyzu1dndyypmhbtbplrfro.
8. http://blog.hubspot.com/marketing/visual-content-marketing-strategy#sm.00000k3rixxv99cnlrkxj94gno6a1.
9. http://www.cmo.com/features/articles/2014/3/10/mind_blowing_stats_slideshare.html.

Chapter 23

1. https://www.jfklibrary.org/Research/Research-Aids/Ready-Reference/JFK-Quotations/Inaugural-Address.aspx.

INDEX

for Befriender, 41
for Captivator, 51
for Creator, 60–61
for Curator, 70
for Demonstrator, 80–81
for Director, 90–91
for Educator, 100–101
for Liberator, 110–111
for Navigator, 120–121
for Performer, 131
for Producer, 141
for Scholar, 151
for Scientist, 160–161
for Soldier, 171
Eye contact
    Navigator advice for, 126
    Scholar advice for, 156
    Scientist advice for, 166

F

Facebook, 247–248
Failure, 243
Fear
    Captivator lack of, 54
    Creator lack of, 63
    of Curator, 72–73, 76
    of Navigator, 120, 122, 124, 126
    of Scholar, 153
    of Scientist, 163–164
    of Sharing, 213
Feedback, 11
    for authenticity, 212
    Liberator need for, 113
    Navigator advice for, 126
    Scientist advice for, 166
    360 review for, 212
Ferriss, Tim, 243–244
Fine Roast coffee beans, 42–43
Follow-up materials
    Activator advice for, 27
    ideal Director use of, 97
    ideal Navigator use of, 127
    ideal Performer use of, 137
    Scientist use of, 163–164, 166
Franklin, Ben, 237

G

GettGysburg Address (Lincoln), 238
GlowShow tech company, 22–23
Glucksberg, Sam, 187

Goals
    Demonstrator long-term creation of, 87
    Director regarding, 94, 97
    Educator expansion of, 107
    list for, 252–253
    Scholar clarity needed for, 153
    Soldier long-term, 169–170
Grit, 14–15
Ground Zero speech (Bush), 220–221
Group activity
    Demonstrator advice for, 86
    Educator asset of, 103
    Navigator inclination towards, 120
    Producer advice for, 146–147
Growth, 181–183

H

Harry Potter (Rowling), 228–229
Harvard Business Review, 213
Headphone corporation, 152–153
Honesty, 11
Honeybee project, 32–33, 38
Humor
    Performer regarding, 134, 136
    Producer advice for, 146

I

Influence, 24
Information
    Curator regarding, 73, 77
    Educator excess of, 104–105
    for introduction method, 232
    Scholar strength of, 154
    Scientist excess of, 163, 167
    Soldier excessive focus on, 170
Inspiration, 33, 233–234
Interaction
    Activator advice for, 26
    Advocator skill of, 29
    Curator cultivation of, 73–74, 77
    Demonstrator regarding, 86, 87–88
    Educator regarding, 103, 107
    Performer ease of, 129
    Producer avoidance of, 139–140, 143
Introduction methods, 231–232
IQ, 14–15
Ironman, 11–12

J

Jobs, Steve
    Exploration mastery by, 188
    key word strategy of, 217
Jupe Verte, 52–53, 57

ABOUT THE AUTHORS

 SCOTT SCHWERTLY is the founder and CEO of Ethos3, an award-winning presentation training and design company with national and international clients ranging from Fortune 500 companies to some of today's biggest thought leaders. Ethos3 has served almost 600 clients in 20 countries, and it has designed more than 1,300 presentations.

When Scott is not working with his team building presentations, you will find him in the pool, on the bike, or on a long run since he is a two-time Ironman, six-time marathoner, and competitive triathlete. He has a BA and MBA from Harding University.

Scott lives in Nashville, Tennessee, with his wife, son, and two dogs.

 SUNDAY MANCINI is a former content strategist at Ethos3, with many years of presentation-writing experience. She helps some of America's biggest brands tell their stories. An avid reader, fan of orange cats, and craft beer devotee, she has a BA in writing from the University of Redlands.

Sunday lives in Nashville, Tennessee.